IMAGES
of America

SISTERS OF CHARITY
OF SETON HILL

*In anticipation of our
150th Anniversary Year
(August 2020-August 2021)
we share with you this pictorial review
highlighting moments and ministries
of our congregation's life.*

*We hope you enjoy the book
and the memories it evokes,
for you have shared
in our life and mission.*

SISTERS OF CHARITY OF SETON HILL

144 DePaul Center Road • Greensburg, PA 15601 • 724.836.0406
www.scsh.org

IMAGES
of America

SISTERS OF CHARITY
OF SETON HILL

Casey Bowser and
Sr. Louise Grundish, SC

ARCADIA
PUBLISHING

Published by Arcadia Publishing
Charleston, South Carolina

Printed in the United States of America

Library of Congress Control Number: 2019931733

For all general information, please contact Arcadia Publishing:
Telephone 843-853-2070
Fax 843-853-0044
E-mail sales@arcadiapublishing.com
For customer service and orders:
Toll-Free 1-888-313-2665

Visit us on the Internet at www.arcadiapublishing.com

*This volume is dedicated to all of the spiritual daughters of
St. Elizabeth Ann Seton . . . past, present, and future.*

CONTENTS

ACKNOWLEDGMENTS

The authors must thank the unwavering and vital support of the Sisters of Charity of Seton Hill provincial superior, Sr. Catherine Meinert, as well as her council. In addition, Sr. Sung-hae Kim, general superior, and her council, thank you for taking a chance on this project. Thanks is also given to the Korean provincial superior, Sr. Yong Son Kim, as well as her council.

We thank Erin Vosgien, Caitrin Cunningham, and Ryan Vied from Arcadia for their assistance. Much appreciation goes to Bill Black, Seton Hill University archivist, and to Dennis Wodzinski, archivist for the Diocese of Pittsburgh, for their assistance with photographs and keen fact-checking abilities. Thanks is owed to Bridget Malley, archival intern, for her advice and editing skills. Finally, we thank Srs. Brigid Marie Grandey, Vivien Linkhauer, and Mary Catherine Seli for reviewing the manuscript. All images, unless otherwise noted, are courtesy of the Sisters of Charity of Seton Hill Archives.

To the donors and benefactors of the Sisters of Charity of Seton Hill, we wholeheartedly appreciate your support for the missions and care of the sisters. All of this rich history would not be possible without you.

Casey would like to thank Mom, Dad, and Chloe for their wisdom and support. Infinite love is given to Andy and Eleanor for making me smile every day.

Sister Louise would like to thank God for the call to religious life and the opportunity to share the life and history of the Sisters of Charity in the areas of nursing, teaching, leadership, and archives for more than 67 years.

Finally, to all of the Sisters of Charity of Seton Hill, you are not only inspiring women religious, but also truly kind and generous spirits. To many of us—the orphaned infant, the mother in the maternity ward, the wide-eyed second grade child, the poor immigrant, the elderly veteran with cancer, the university student struggling with faith—you are a hero. We thank you.

INTRODUCTION

A young woman born in New York on the cusp of the American Revolution would grow to inspire a movement equally as groundbreaking. Elizabeth Ann Seton became the founder of the Sisters of Charity, the first American congregation of religious sisters in the United States in 1809. What is her story, and why do we still feel her presence in the world?

A wealthy and educated Elizabeth was raised with great devotion in the Episcopal Church, but she often considered the works of great theologians and philosophers in other faith traditions. She had complex convictions, to say the least. Marriage and motherhood enlivened Elizabeth and brought new perspectives to her worldview.

After tumbling from a position of wealth and status into the depths of poverty and despair, Elizabeth struggled in her relationship with God. She lost her husband to tuberculosis while on a trip to Italy. Elizabeth made her conversion of heart and mind in the beautiful, historic locale of Livorno, Italy. She would become a Catholic.

On her return from Europe, Elizabeth Ann Seton was received into the Catholic Church on March 14, 1805, at the age of 31. Friends and family disowned her. She had five children and no steady income. With the help of her Catholic friends and priests, Elizabeth initially pursued a teaching vocation. God, however, was calling her to a higher vocation.

At the urging of Rev. Louis William Dubourg, SS, and Bishop John Carroll, of Baltimore, Elizabeth formally established a religious community in Emmitsburg, Maryland, in 1809. First, they opened St. Joseph's Academy and Free School where paid academy students subsidized the education of poor, young Catholic girls. In 1655, the Bishop of Paris gave permission for St. Vincent De Paul and St. Louise DeMarillac to write *Common Rules of the Daughters of Charity* for the French Daughters of Charity. It was published in 1672. Mother Seton's early sisters adapted *Common Rules of the Daughters of Charity* and lived a Vincentian life in service of the poor. Missions expanded beyond education to include orphanages and infirmaries, among other social service institutions.

Elizabeth died in 1821 at the age of 46. She encountered much hardship and heartache throughout her short life, but the success of her small community filled her with immense joy. Her sisters loved "Mother," and her legacy would live on. Independent communities expanded to New York (1846); Cincinnati (1852); Halifax, Nova Scotia (1856); New Jersey (1859); and Greensburg, Pennsylvania (1870).

Generations of Americans young and old, Catholic and non-Catholic, poor and rich, have benefited from Elizabeth's vision for the world. Mother Seton's spiritual daughters, infused with the Setonian charism, have continued and broadened the missions of those first sisters in Emmitsburg. Charism, as a special gift of the Holy Spirit, imbues members of the Catholic Church to work on behalf of Christ for the good of all humankind. The Vincentian-Setonian charism not only infuses and strengthens the congregation, it also becomes manifest in the various missions of the sisters.

The significance of Mother Seton's legacy culminated in her sainthood acknowledged on September 14, 1975, by Pope Paul VI. Thousands of sisters and lay devotees around the world were finally granted the recognition of Elizabeth's holy life and eternal reward. How have Mother Seton's daughters sustained this magnificent legacy? The Sisters of Charity of Seton Hill are but one example of the Vincentian-Setonian charism at work.

Founded in August 1870, the Sisters of Charity of Seton Hill settled in Altoona at the foothills of the Allegheny Mountains in Western Pennsylvania. The Catholic Church in the region was young and ripe for expansion as Irish, German, and Eastern European immigrants flocked to burgeoning new cities. King Coal, Queen Coke, and Princess Steel were about to ascend the throne in Pittsburgh and its suburbs. As populations boomed and Catholic priests envisioned flourishing church communities and parish schools, the need for women religious became apparent.

When Mother Aloysia Lowe and her five companions arrived in Altoona, the parishioners of St. John the Evangelist Church welcomed them with great fanfare. A line of people waved and cheered as their carriage paraded through town. The children's choir presented a special, private concert for the sisters. Although the welcome was warm, anti-Catholic sentiment persisted among the general population.

Missions expanded to Blairsville and Pittsburgh. Mother Aloysia, recognizing the rapid growth of the region and of the community, began searching for a new, permanent home for the sisters. In 1882, she purchased the 200-acre Jennings farm on a scenic hilltop in Greensburg, Pennsylvania, the seat of Westmoreland County. Positioned near the Pennsylvania Railroad, the farmland property benefited from the hustle and bustle of a growing Greensburg and provided convenient transportation needed for the increasing missionary work.

St. Mary's School for Boys and St. Joseph's Academy for Girls were established as the sisters' independent flagship schools in Greensburg. As the schools flourished, Mother Aloysia dedicated her remaining days to the building of a new motherhouse at Seton Hill. She hired and fired contractors. She measured door frames and assessed window glass. Mother Aloysia's keen business acumen and attention to detail served the community well. St. Joseph's Motherhouse and Academy became the crowning jewel of Greensburg.

By the time Mother Aloysia passed into eternal rest in 1889, the community included 156 sisters and 16 different missions. Her protégé, Sr. Ann Regina Ennis, succeeded Mother Aloysia as mother superior. The congregation's great work continued. Mother Ann Regina witnessed the expansion into health care in 1891 with the establishment of Roselia Foundling and Maternity Hospital. Pittsburgh Hospital would follow a few years later.

Mother Josephine Doran brought the community into the 20th century. In 1908, the Sisters of Charity established two important missions, Pittsburgh's DePaul Institute, a school for deaf and hard of hearing children, and Providence Hospital in Beaver Falls, which was the sisters' third hospital facility. The educational missions, particularly in neighborhoods of Pittsburgh, continued with steady growth into the 1920s. In a pioneering move, the Sisters of Charity of Seton Hill volunteered to teach black Sisters of the Holy Family in segregated and racially charged New Orleans, Louisiana, in 1921.

St. Joseph's Academy, which had forged an exemplary reputation for cultivating young women since 1883, offered junior college courses in 1914. By 1918, Sr. Francesca Brownlee, directress, earned the charter for an institution of higher education, Seton Hill College. St. Joseph's Academy would continue educating young women for the world until its formal closing in 1947.

The Sisters of Charity and Seton Hill College, now University, maintained a close relationship over the past century. Most sisters earned their undergraduate degree at Seton Hill. Many young women first encountered the community while enrolled at the college and later chose to enter religious life. Up until the 1960s, sisters comprised the majority of the staff and faculty of the college. Together, the students, lay staff and faculty, and sisters shared their love of Seton Hill.

The Great Depression forced economic hardships on both the sisters and the missions in which they worked. The mother superiors accepted only one new mission between 1926 and

1940, and it was a providential one. Mother M. Eveline Fisher made the momentous choice to send the Sisters of Charity of Seton Hill to the American Southwest in 1933. It was the first real missionary work of the sisters—the climate, environment, language, and people were quite foreign to these Western Pennsylvanians.

The 1940s and 1950s exhibited the growth of the Catholic Church in America as schools were founded from new and growing parishes. After the Great Depression and war years, the sisters developed social service programs to meet the needs of individual communities. The sisters also witnessed an influx of applicants to the novitiate of the community. For many Catholics, it was a great honor to have a "sister" in the family.

The second true pioneering effort of the Sisters of Charity began in 1960 when Mother Claudia Glenn made the pivotal decision to send four missionaries to Korea. Providence from God must have been at work because the Korean community now boasts around 200 sisters ministering to the lowest and yet, greatest, among us.

As society and the Catholic Church changed, so too have the sisters. The implications of Vatican II became real in the 1960s through the 1970s and beyond. The sisters, traditionally in black habit and cap, modified their dress. The liturgy was transformed. Community life was redefined. For some sisters, change was due. To others, it was a shock.

Nevertheless, the sisters persisted and continued the more traditional work in education and health care while also beginning to attend to other underserved communities. These diversified ministries offered nontraditional education to children in poor neighborhoods, opportunities to serve immigrants and refugees, the ability to help prisoners and those with devastating disease, and a means to express creativity or develop a professional career in an unconventional field. These were, and are, women living the motto "*Caritas Christi Urget Nos,*" meaning "the Charity of Christ Urges Us." From the classroom to the hospital bed, from the child's First Communion to the adult's need for spiritual guidance, from the prison cell to the refugee camp, from Pittsburgh to Korea, the sisters exhibit charity, humility, simplicity, and God's presence in daily life. Those moved by these acts of pure love are endowed with the power of this charism and do great good for others.

Women religious in America are rarely given credit for the vital role they have played in founding and sustaining major institutions. These were women who built schools, hospitals, parishes, and nonprofits from the ground up. These were women pursuing educational opportunities and equal rights before the passage of the Nineteenth Amendment. These were women of the Catholic Church in America, and they have voices worth hearing and experiences worth remembering.

This volume serves not only as a nostalgic look back at the tireless work of one community of Mother Seton's daughters, but also represents the way forward.

Hazard yet forward!

Sr. Fides Glass, a prolific artist, writer, and illustrator, completed this portrait of Elizabeth Ann Seton in 1944. The background shows the original Stone House of Mother Seton's community. Sister Fides modeled Elizabeth's face from the study of a 1794 miniature painted for Elizabeth's husband, William. Sister Fides, born in 1889 in Cresson, Pennsylvania, entered the Sisters of Charity in 1908. She graduated from the Carnegie Institute of Technology in 1930. In addition to her art, Sister Fides studied and wrote about Prince Demetrius Gallitzin, known as the Apostle of the Alleghenies, and Elizabeth Ann Seton. She was an early champion of Elizabeth Seton's cause for canonization.

One

A HOME FOR THE SISTERS

A growing Catholic population in Altoona impelled Rev. John Tuigg, pastor of St. John the Evangelist Church, to ask Bishop Michael Domenec, the second bishop of the Diocese of Pittsburgh, for a religious community to guide the educational and spiritual well-being of the students of St. John's School in 1869. The bishop appealed to the Sisters of Charity of Cincinnati to establish a new community of sisters in the Diocese of Pittsburgh.

On August 20, 1870, Srs. Aloysia Lowe, Blanche O'Keefe, Maria Teresa O'Donnell, and Maria Kavanaugh arrived in Altoona with two young novices. In less than two weeks, they welcomed the students of St. John's School. Sister Aloysia was installed by the Cincinnati council as the first mother superior of the new community. In 1873, Rev. James Stillinger enlisted the sisters to staff SS. Simon and Jude School in Blairsville, and shortly thereafter, they founded St. Mary's School for Boys.

The good work of the sisters began to reach neighborhoods of bustling, industrial Pittsburgh. Young girls, eager to dedicate themselves to God's work, daydreamed of donning the black cap of a Sister of Charity. Mother Aloysia recognized the signs of imminent expansion, not only of the religious community, but of the Catholic parochial school system and, thereby, the great need of women religious throughout Western Pennsylvania.

In 1882, Mother Aloysia found the perfect seat for her young community—the 200-acre Jennings farm in Greensburg. It was purchased for $75,000.

Anxious to begin a new life in Greensburg, Mother Aloysia put the name and location of the new motherhouse to a vote with the sisters. Would it be "Villa Maria" in the glen or "Seton Hill" on the crest? The answer was nearly unanimous.

The sisters transferred St. Mary's School for Boys to Seton Hill and began conducting St. Joseph's Academy for Girls in 1883. Schools of music and art were also offered in Greensburg. Mother Aloysia focused on the building of an imposing new motherhouse and academy facility. This architectural gem would serve many purposes over the years but would come to represent the beating heart of a mission Mother Aloysia perhaps never dreamed of, a thriving institution of higher education for young women, Seton Hill College.

Bishop Michael Domenec, second bishop of Pittsburgh, was consecrated and installed as bishop on December 9, 1860. He was a member of the Congregation of the Mission (Vincentian). In God's providence, a Vincentian priest would be responsible for the presence of the Sisters of Charity in Pittsburgh. In 1876, he became bishop of Allegheny and resigned that appointment in 1877. He died in Spain on January 5, 1878. (Courtesy of the Archives and Records Center of the Diocese of Pittsburgh.)

Fr. John Tuigg, pastor of St. John parish, who had urged Bishop Domenec to seek the establishment of the sisters in the diocese, boarded the train to welcome Mother Aloysia Lowe and her companions on August 20, 1870. The Angelus bell rang as he led the procession of pioneers from the depot to the convent where lighted candles glowed from every window. Father Tuigg was consecrated and installed as the third bishop of Pittsburgh in 1876. Following a series of strokes, he died on December 7, 1889. During the last months of his final illness, four Sisters of Charity ministered to him day and night.

Mother Aloysia Lowe (right) served as mother superior from 1870 until 1889. She oversaw the staffing of over 15 Catholic schools in Western Pennsylvania, including the founding of St. Joseph's Academy. In addition, she was the driving force behind the move from Altoona to Greensburg in 1882. In the years before her death in 1889, Mother Aloysia focused on the building of an imposing new motherhouse and academy facility in Greensburg. As the assistant mother and mistress of novices, Sr. Ann Regina (below) played an essential role in the functioning of the community. She later succeeded Mother Aloysia and helped establish Roselia Foundling and Maternity Asylum in Pittsburgh. Unfortunately, Mother Ann Regina's tenure was cut short. After suffering from a tumor for over a year, Mother Regina opted for elective surgery to remove it. She died unexpectedly as a result of the surgery in 1894.

When the sisters began St. John's School in 1870, a total of 300 children were in attendance. St. John's Academy was a separate paid school implemented for the older female students in Altoona. These young women received instruction in literature, mathematics, and language, as well as needlework, music, and painting. Pictured here is Sr. Geraldine Fardy with students of St. John's School.

St. John's School, shown here around 1916, would become known as Cathedral School after 1924, when the original building was replaced with the Cathedral of the Blessed Sacrament. It would later become McNelis Catholic, which would merge with the Altoona Central Catholic Schools. Sisters of Charity would serve as principal from 1870 until 1988. One hundred young women from Altoona, including students of St. John's School, entered the Sisters of Charity.

Fr. James A. Stillinger, first pastor of SS. Simon and Jude Church, wrote Mother Aloysia to request sisters to teach the parish children. Father Stillinger received his education at St. Mary's Seminary in Emmitsburg and knew of Elizabeth Ann Seton and her great work in Catholic education. He was anxious to have her sisters as teachers in his parish. Mother Aloysia accompanied four sisters to Blairsville on January 7, 1873. Father Stillinger was pastor from 1830 until his death on September 18, 1873.

FIRST MISSION - 1873
SS. SIMON and JUDE, BLAIRSVILLE
(l) Sr. Mary Cecilia Brown, Fr. Francis Brady,
(r) Sr. Vincentia Volk
(photograph c. 1890)

Srs. Mary Cecilia Brown (standing left) and Vincentia Wolk (standing right) pose with students of SS. Simon and Jude School in the 1890s. Fr. Francis Brady, an early assistant at the parish and the third pastor from 1889 to 1897, sits in the first row, fourth from the left.

This photograph of the interior of the first permanent SS. Simon and Jude Church dates after 1858 when Father Stillinger enhanced the interior of church with nine oil paintings by Franz Xaver Glink, a noted German artist. Four of these oil paintings are visible in the photograph. This church served the parish until replaced by a new structure in 1973.

The Sisters of Charity at St. Mary's Convent in Blairsville welcomed William, Edward, and James McKeever into the convent following the death of their mother in the late fall of 1880. The third floor of the convent became a boarding school. From this humble beginning, St. Mary's School for Boys was born. Edward Francis Dunn, age five, whose mother also died, joined the school in 1881. St. Mary's School moved to the old academy building, formerly the Stokes mansion, at Seton Hill in 1889.

When Mother Aloysia purchased the Jennings farm in Greensburg in 1882, the main structure on the property was known as the Stokes mansion. William Axton Stokes, who owned the property from 1847 to 1867, was a Philadelphia lawyer and Civil War major. The Stokes mansion would house the first motherhouse and academy in Greensburg, St. Mary's School for Boys, and later the home economics and theater departments of Seton Hill College.

The sisters opened St. Joseph's Academy for Girls in the Stokes mansion in 1883. Pictured here are, from left to right, Anastasia Casey, Rose Padden, Alice Akers (standing), and Sarah Sullivan, the first graduating class of St. Joseph's Academy in 1887. Sarah Sullivan would join the ranks of the Sisters of Charity shortly after graduation and become Sr. Mary Angela.

Famed Pittsburgh architect Joseph Stillburg designed St. Joseph's Academy and motherhouse. In this original sketch from 1887, one can see that much of Stillburg's vision came to life. Mother Aloysia ensured that every inch of St. Joseph's was up to par. The striking facade of the academy and motherhouse would come to represent a center of Catholic education and community.

This image shows the completed St. Joseph's Academy and motherhouse from about 1890 to 1892. It is believed to be the earliest known photograph of the original building before adjustments were made in 1896 to include a chapel annex.

This pre-1920 photograph of Greensburg was taken from the vantage point of Seton Hill. When Mother Aloysia bought the land in 1882, it was noted that the landscape was akin to the great hills of Rome.

At the St. Joseph's Academy, students were not only taught academic subjects, but these young women needed to learn the lessons of the day, including the painting of fine china. Pictured is an early image of the china studio at the academy.

From left to right, Srs. Maria Francesca Urnauer, M. Francesca Brownlee, and M. Electa Boyle enjoy a day out with students of St. Joseph's Academy. Sr. Maria Francesca emigrated from Germany and taught the language at the school. Sister Francesca was the directress of the academy and first dean of Seton Hill College. Sister Electa was known as an excellent teacher of history and English. She became the first archivist of the community. Each of these women would prove influential in the establishment of Seton Hill College.

The glorious landscape of Seton Hill and the majesty of St. Joseph's Academy created the perfect venue for elaborate plays. The sisters and students of the academy staged magnificent performances that were attended by local Greensburgers. Pictured here is a St. Joseph's Academy student, dressed in metal armor, ready for one such stage play.

Music Class
July 1882

The sisters prepared meals, cleaned the building, tended to the farm, committed to a schedule of prayer, and received their own education within the walls of St. Joseph's. Seen in this photograph of a music class from 1892 are Srs. Beatrice Gority, Angelica Rooney, Marie Joseph Darr, Josephine Doran (Mother), Mary Grace Ryan, Mary Inez Cronin, Annina O'Donnell, Andrea Millbach (withdrew), Mary James Brownlee, DeChantal Brownlee, Hilda Popp, Maria Flanigan, and Felicita McGuire.

St. Joseph's Academy students were able to decorate their rooms just like modern college students. Here, one sees a glimpse into the dorm of a 1912 graduate of the academy.

Recreation was an important part of daily life at St. Mary's School for Boys. The sisters encouraged the boys to engage in baseball, soccer, and swimming in Lake Regina. Pictured are, from left to right, Thomas Nilan, Jack Daily, Alan Mooney, Paul Sheetz, Gerald O'Brien, Victor Ruffner, John Seibert, Edward Barry, and Francis Lawson, the members of St. Mary's 1911 competitive baseball team.

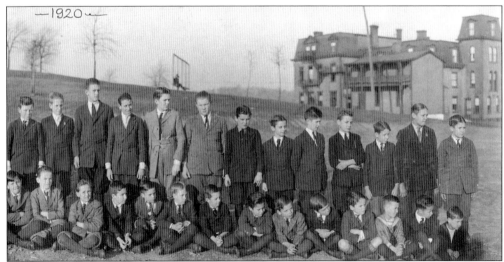

Here is the class of St. Mary's School for Boys in 1920 posing outside of St. Mary's or the Stokes mansion. Many of the boys went on to become politicians, priests, military leaders, and successful businessmen. The names written on the back of the image include Robert Brinker, Maurice Smith, John Roszella, John Shea, Charles Weible, Donald Atkinson, Salvatore Sunncerri, J.W. Irwin, Ed Gallagher, William DuPont, Regis Kelly, Urban Gillespie, and Robert Smith, Thomas Gallagher, Edward Jones, Leo Cauley, Harry Butler, John Reilly, Philip Poet, Harry Longman, Robert Wholey, Alexis Walsh, Charles Cramer, John Felix, and Raymond Mioli. Two of the boys are unidentified.

Two

A Pioneering Spirit

Women religious have always been leaders in the realm of education, health care, social service, and parish ministry, but to forge paths and build institutions in a foreign land would seem a daunting task. The Sisters of Charity of Seton Hill have embraced the pioneering spirit of St. Elizabeth Ann Seton and her religious daughters.

Despite inconvenient travel, harsh climes, new languages, and issues of poverty, racism, and societal instability, the Sisters of Charity of Seton Hill established missions in Louisiana, the American Southwest, and Korea.

In 1921, the Sisters of Charity of Seton Hill were approached by the Catholic Colored Mission Board to teach a congregation of Sisters of the Holy Family in New Orleans, Louisiana. They were the only community to agree to the arrangement. Jim Crow laws prevented black and biracial sisters from earning teaching certification and continuing their own ministries to young African American students. The Sisters of Charity of Seton Hill ignored segregation laws and deep-seated prejudice to offer equal education to black women religious. The summer normal school continued for 30 years, but more importantly, it established a deep and lasting relationship with a sister congregation.

Mother Eveline Fisher sent Sisters of Charity to staff SS. Peter and Paul School in Tucson, Arizona, in 1933. It was the sisters' first foray into the American Southwest. The ministries would multiply to include 12 schools in Tucson, Chandler, Ajo, and Scottsdale, Arizona, and Lakewood, California, and a multitude of social service programs. The West introduced the sisters to work with Native American and Mexican people and produced several vocations for the community.

The Sisters of Charity of Seton Hill became an international congregation with the beginning of their work in Korea in 1960. At the invitation of Archbishop Harold Henry, Mother Claudia Glenn sent Srs. Thomas Aquinas (Mary Agnes) Carey, Mary Noreen Lacey, Marie Timothy (Alice) Ruane, and Martin de Porres Knock to open a school and convent in the Vicariate of Kwangju in South Korea. Little did they know that the foreign mission to Korea would lead to the establishment of a Korean novitiate. This fledgling community has grown into an autonomous province of 200 Korean Sisters of Charity with missions aiding children and adults with physical and mental disabilities, the growth of educational facilities, and the founding of social service and pastoral programs, including two retreat centers and an Interreligious Dialogue Center, throughout the Republic of South Korea, Ecuador, and China.

Founded in 1837 in New Orleans, Louisiana, by Henriette DeLille, the Sisters of the Holy Family had been teaching young black children in the South for nearly seven decades before the Sisters of Charity arrived in 1921. In order to reestablish black religious teachers in Jim Crow–era Louisiana, the Sisters of Charity conducted a summer normal school from 1921 until 1957. Pictured are six Sisters of Charity with a summer cohort of nearly 60 Sisters of the Holy Family in the 1930s.

The sisters taught English, history with geography, catechism and Bible history, Palmer Method, and sight singing in the early years. For most of the 30 years in New Orleans, the Sisters of Charity were forced to live with another white congregation of women religious due to racial segregation. Over 50 Sisters of Charity would go to New Orleans to teach as part of the summer school program.

Sister Benjamin Auzenne, S.S.F.
Sociology

Beginning in 1942, the Sisters of Charity of Seton Hill offered scholarships to Seton Hill College for Sisters of the Holy Family. This agreement was a generous extension of the work the sisters had done in New Orleans but was also evidence of the great relationship between congregations of two different races in the midst of social and racial conflict. Seventeen Sisters of the Holy Family earned their undergraduate degree from the college. (Courtesy of Seton Hill University Archives.)

In 1967, a faculty exchange program was implemented between the schools of the Sisters of Charity and the Sisters of the Holy Family in order to combat racial prejudice and integrate students and faculty. Pictured are Srs. Rita Marie Hokamp (left) and Frances Augustine (fourth from left) with the faculty of St. Paul the Apostle School in New Orleans in 1969. The program lasted until 1980.

25

Mother Eveline Fisher made the visionary decision to send the first group of sisters to Tucson, Arizona, in 1933. Pictured in front of the first convent in Tucson are members of the original cohort, which included Srs. Emily Miller, Cecelia Vincent McCartney, Francis Mary Coleman, Rose Catherine Ward, M. Ermanilda Knepley, M. Estelle Hensler, Mary Inez Clark, and James Marie Malone.

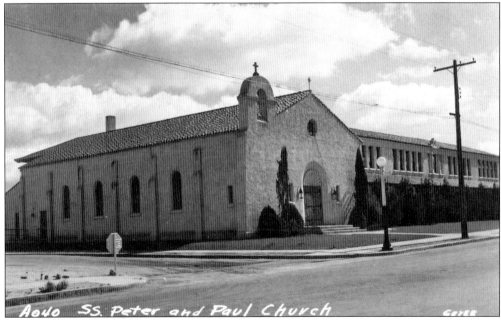

Fr. Joseph Patterson and Fr. Leo Gattes contacted Mother Eveline to staff SS. Peter and Paul School in Tucson. Pictured here is the church built in 1931. Although Arizona was not the Wild West of lore, the landscape, culture, language, and lifestyle of the area proved a difficult adjustment for the Western Pennsylvania sisters.

In addition to their parochial school work, the pioneer sisters began conducting catechetical courses for Spanish-speaking Mexican immigrant children in places like the Yaqui Indian Village, Nogales, and Solomonville, Arizona. Pictured are Srs. Helen Louise Connelly (left) and Estelle Hensler (right) with a 1930s summer Confraternity of Christian Doctrine (CCD) class in Solomonville.

The second mission of the Sisters of Charity in Arizona was technically at St. John the Evangelist parish in Tucson, where the sisters began catechetical work in 1934. They began the school in 1950. Pictured are Srs. LaSalette Hays, Remigius Betz, and Mary Antonia Ward overseeing an outdoor lunch at St. John the Evangelist School in 1953.

Over 85 Sisters of Charity served at St. John the Evangelist School from 1950 until the community withdrew in 1995. Sr. Harold Ann Jones was the last of a long line of Sister of Charity principals at St. John in Tucson.

Salpointe, a central Catholic high school opened by the Diocese of Tucson in September 1950, was staffed by a combination of women religious, priests, and lay staff. Sr. Maria Magdalen (Marian) McKelvey, high school guidance director, chats with a senior about college choices in the early 1960s.

In 1953, the Sisters of Charity purchased the old Potter School, a tremendous residence that had previously served as a college preparatory school, in Tucson to accommodate Casa Elizabeth Seton, a western novitiate for postulants of the order, and a new kindergarten.

Casa Elizabeth Seton kindergarten became known for its excellent reputation under the tutelage of Sr. Christine Marie McElhinny. In this 1960s photograph, kindergarten students present flowers before a statue of St. Elizabeth Ann Seton. The school closed in 1972 when kindergarten became part of the public school system in Arizona.

The Sisters of Charity of Seton Hill brought the story of Mother Seton to the people of Arizona. In 1959, Casa Elizabeth Seton students participated in the annual Tucson rodeo parade in full costume to celebrate the 150th anniversary of the parochial school system in America, as developed by Elizabeth Seton.

In 1942, Srs. Suzanne McIntyre and Dominica O'Connor were missioned to Ajo, a small mining town on the Arizona-Mexico border, to conduct CCD classes. Fr. George Feeney asked the sisters to commit to year-round teaching in Immaculate Conception parish. Since many of the children spoke Spanish or Papago-Pima, an Uto-Aztecan indigenous language, the sisters initially struggled to communicate with their students.

Much of the real missionary work of the sisters was conducted in Ajo in places like the St. Catherine Indian Mission. Here, one sees, from left to right, Srs. Rita Catherine Cole, Mary Timothy Adams, Mary Peter Murphy, Helen Marie Haley, and Harold Ann Jones with Fr. Regis Rhoder, Order of Friars Minor (OFM), with a vacation school class in 1948. Mexican Catholics would cross the border by the hundreds to receive baptism and confirmation from American priests assisted by the Sisters of Charity.

In 1952, Sr. Agnes Vincent Brazill was encouraged to start a kindergarten at Immaculate Conception parish in Ajo. It would eventually turn into an eight-grade parochial school. Local mining strikes of the late 1960s and changes in parish leadership forced Immaculate Conception School to close in 1972, but the catechetical work of the sisters did continue for several more years.

The Sisters of Charity of Seton Hill were recruited by Father Patterson, formerly of SS. Peter and Paul parish, to join him at St. Mary's parish in Chandler in 1944. In order to fulfill the spiritual and educational needs of Hispanic children neglected by segregated public schools, a school was built next to St. Mary's Church.

Sr. Mary Norbert Long, the last Sister of Charity to serve St. Mary-Basha School as principal, left her position as superintendent of the Tucson Catholic Schools in 1984 and served as principal until 2012. In 1994, St. Mary-Basha received the prestigious National Blue Ribbon School award by the US Department of Education, the highest honor presented to elementary schools.

Seton High School in Chandler opened in 1954 and later became a tri-parish school. The Madden sisters were, perhaps, two of the most influential staff at Seton. Sr. Mary Ronald Madden, pictured at center with students, served as the first principal of the high school. Sr. Joan Marie Madden worked as teacher, librarian, and registrar for over 41 years.

In 1962, the Sisters of the West changed their habits from black to white. Desert dust and heat made real mission work uncomfortable in the black habit. The change created a stir among parishioners and students. In this photograph from the 1960s, Srs. Jean Agnes (Irene) Fallon (left) and Olivia Hamilton (right) don their new habits as they offer a cup of water to Butch Culling as he helps to build the new St. Catherine of Siena School in Phoenix.

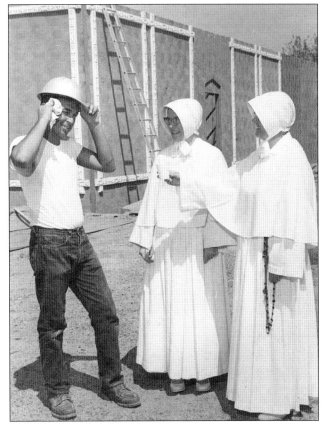

In 1949, the Sisters of Charity began to staff St. Catherine of Siena School in Phoenix, Arizona. Pictured here are the faculty in the 1960s, including, from left to right, Srs. John Patrick (Eleanor) Gibbons, Mary Nicholas Matro, Olivia Hamilton, Marie Goretti Kleman, Kathleen Dorman, and Esther Marie Phillips. The community withdrew from the school in 1988.

The sisters' work at St. Catherine's parish in Phoenix extended to the San Carlos Indian Mission. Pictured is the mission church and the summer school hall where the sisters taught young Apache children about the Catholic faith.

St. Theresa School was the second mission in Phoenix. Srs. Macaria Nestor, Mary Michael Burns, and Marie Margaret Wolf, along with a lay teacher, Mrs. Ganz, comprised the staff for the opening year in 1957. Shown are Srs. Marie Margaret and Mary Michael welcoming three little girls at the front entrance of St. Theresa School.

Between 1957 and 1992, fifty-eight Sisters of Charity served as teachers and principals of St. Theresa in Phoenix. Sr. Marie Veronica Gogolin was the last principal. Pictured is a rear view of St. Theresa School and its playground with Camelback Mountain looming in the background.

Mother Claudia Glenn, who had founded four new missions in the West in seven years, sent sisters to Our Lady of Perpetual Help (OLPH) parish and school in Scottsdale, Arizona, in 1956. Over 90 Sisters of Charity shared their gifts with the students of OLPH. Sr. Ida Catherine Sullivan poses with the third grade class of Our Lady of Perpetual Help in 1967.

Sr. Ann Christopher (Joan) Winters escorts Our Lady of Perpetual Help students onto the school bus at the end of a hot day in 1963.

St. Daniel the Prophet School in Scottsdale, Arizona, was established in 1963 and originally guided by the Sisters of St. Dominic. The school struggled with low enrollment. When that congregation withdrew, Sr. Mary Lucilla Wertz (center), of the Seton Hill community, commanded the reins. Under Sister Mary Lucilla's administration, academic scores began to rise, sports programs were initiated, and the Catholic spirit of the community became manifest in an educational setting.

After some years in Arizona, the sisters were able to also extend their mission work to Lakewood, California, in 1955. Srs. Mary Amy Connolly, Macaria Nestor, Rose Catherine Ward, Ethelreda Merz, Marie Kathleen Galvin, and Mary Michael Burns were among the first faculty at St. Pancratius School. Pictured are Srs. Mary Michael, Suzanne McIntyre, Amy Connelly, and Macaria Nestor on the convent patio.

Although the Sisters of Charity formally withdrew from St. Pancratius in 1985, Sr. Kathleen Dorman returned to serve students in California in the 1990s. She was their gifted teacher, their kind protector, and a friendly, smiling face on the campus until her retirement in 2001.

Continuing the work done in Pittsburgh at DePaul Institute, the Sisters of Charity conducted catechetical courses for blind and deaf students in Tucson in the 1930s. Father Patterson would drive a bus every weekend from the State School for the Deaf and Blind to transport students for Sunday Mass and catechism classes taught by the sisters at SS. Peter and Paul. Pictured are Srs. Rose Catherine Ward (left) and Agnes Marie Reuber (right) with their students.

The Sisters of Charity were particularly concerned for the forgotten populations, including sick children and the elderly. Here, Sr. Ann Augusta Schroth visits children at the Comstock Hospital for Crippled Children. The sisters also visited with children at the Tuberculosis Preventorium.

At the end of vacation school in the summer of 1941, one sees a group of Yaqui Indian children in Nogales, Arizona, making their First Communion. Srs. Harold Ann Jones and James Marie Malone dedicated their time as educators and spiritual guides for this group of children.

On Pentecost Sunday 1959, Mother Claudia Glenn pulled four names out of a selection of 70 Sister of Charity volunteers to begin the new mission in Korea. From left to right, Srs. Mary Agnes Carey, Mary Noreen Lacey, Alice Ruane, and Martin de Porres Knock were the chosen four. The sisters felt called to establish their first foreign mission, in part, because of the excitement surrounding the veneration of Elizabeth Ann Seton that same year.

After a departure ceremony at the cathedral in Greensburg, the four missionaries departed for San Francisco to board a freighter, called the *California Bear*, on October 6. Despite encountering a typhoon and a bull loose on the ship, the sisters completed their journey and arrived in Inchon, Korea, on November 4, 1960.

WELCOME TO KOREA

When the sisters arrived in Mokpo, their anticipated destination, on November 6, they were greeted by local Korean Catholics from Kyong Dong parish with great fanfare. In the five years prior to the arrival of the Sisters of Charity, Korea had experienced an explosion of Catholic conversion, gaining nearly 50 percent more faithful.

In the first weeks in Korea, Sisters Mary Agnes, Alice, Mary Noreen, and Martin de Porres lived with the Irish Columban sisters but moved to a convent hosted by native Caritas sisters. Pictured are Fr. Desmond Maguire of the Missionary Society of St. Columban; the four missionaries; Sisters Albina, Anastasia, and Fides of the Caritas community; and Bishop Harold Henry with his secretary outside of the Caritas convent in Mokpo.

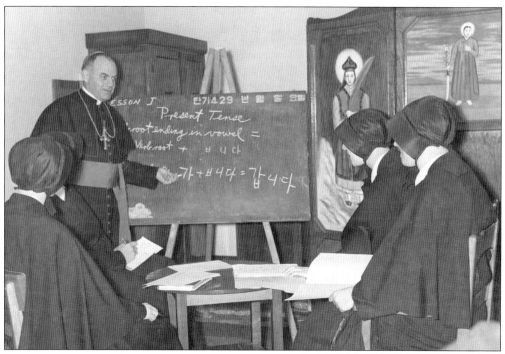

On the chalkboard:
ESSON J 단기4429 년 몇 월 몇 요일
Present Tense
root ending in vowel =
Verb root + ㅂ 니 다
가 + ㅂ니다 = 갑니다

Although the Sisters of Charity had spent months preparing for life in Korea, the first year was dedicated not only to establishing a school, but also to learning Korean language and culture. In this photograph from 1960, Bishop Harold Henry is giving the missionaries a lesson in the Korean language.

The original plan was to establish a school for girls in Mokpo, a port city in the southwestern tip of South Korea with a steady influx of Yellow Sea islanders. Financial and legal difficulties plagued this plan. In the meantime, a run-down school and property in the poor village of Kang Tjin was offered to Archbishop Harold Henry. Their fate was decided. The sisters began to pack their belongings for the move to Kang Tjin.

Extensive renovations were required at the former Kum Nueng School in Kang Tjin. The sisters became familiar with architecture and building practices while they prepared their courses for approval with the Korean Ministry of Education. Here, Sr. Mary Noreen Lacey is chatting with two female construction workers. Although the methods and materials seemed primitive by American standards, the people of the Cholla Nam Do province built an effective school.

When complete, St. Joseph's School housed a middle school and high school for girls. The student population was mostly Confucian, with some Buddhist and a small percent of Catholics, but it filled a great need in the community. Some students traveled from miles away to attend the new school staffed by a team of Sisters of Charity and lay Koreans.

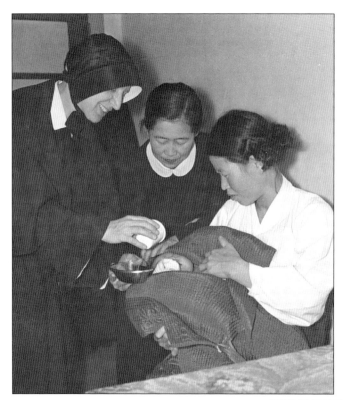

While the sisters oversaw
the completion of the new
St. Joseph's School, they
continued catechetical,
pastoral, and social service
ministries. In these pictures
from the early 1960s, Sr. Mary
Agnes Carey baptizes an
infant, and Sr. Mary Noreen
Lacey adjusts the veil of
Julia Kim in preparation
for Holy Communion.

St. Joseph's School offered traditional high school courses, like language and mathematics, as well as practical courses for young women, including sewing and cooking. Recreation, such as sports and dancing, were also part of the curriculum. Here, Kim Sang-soo is teaching agriculture to first-year St. Joseph's students in 1962.

To encourage the students of St. Joseph's to learn English, Sr. Alice Ruane established a pen pal program with students from Sister of Charity schools in Pittsburgh.

With the growth of St. Joseph's School came the need for more sisters. In November 1962, Srs. Jean Malloy (left) and Jeremy Mahla (right) departed for Korea with the blessing of Msgr. Cyril Vogel (center), vicar general for the Diocese of Greensburg.

In 1965, the first two native Koreans entered the Sisters of Charity of Seton Hill. These young women were graduates of the Jesuit Sogang University. Postulants Myong-he Sohn (left) and Sung-hae Kim (right) study with Mother Victoria Brown. The sisters began their postulancy in Korea but came to the United States for the remainder of their formation. Sr. Sung-hae Kim persevered in religious life and became a teacher. After graduating from Harvard, she served as a professor at Jesuit Sogang University. She was the first Korean general superior of the Sisters of Charity of Seton Hill, which is also governed by two provincial superiors.

In order to support the mission in Korea, the sisters in the United States started a Korean Card Party fundraiser. In this publicity photograph for the party for 1969, Catherine Lee, graduate of St. Joseph's High School and student of Seton Hill College, is bowing to Srs. Patricia Marie Stack (center) and Jeremy Mahla (right). The Sisters of Charity have made a concerted effort to be a truly international congregation.

A separate Korean novitiate was established in 1972. The Korean Region, as a formal entity of the Sisters of Charity, was founded in 1976 with Sr. Mary Agnes Carey as regional superior. Construction of houses of formation took place in 1976 and 1986. This photograph shows the formation/regional house in Pon-Chon Dong, Kwangju, Korea, in 1990. The late 1980s and early 1990s witnessed increasing numbers of Catholic Korean women entering the convent. The community now numbers around 200 sisters.

The community in Korea has grown beyond St. Joseph's School to include Eun-hae School for Children with Physical Disabilities, St. Mary's School for the Blind, Seton House of Studies, pastoral ministry and retreat houses, day-care services, social service programs, refugee assistance, and much more. Sr. Sun-ok Park is pictured with students and parents at Seton Early Education Center, the precursor to Eun-hae School, in 1982.

American Sisters of Charity, like Sr. Mary Michael Burns, have volunteered time in Korea as English teachers for students, teachers, and native Korean sisters. In addition, Korean sisters have come to the United States to study at Seton Hill University, to experience a Mother Seton pilgrimage, and to gain experience in the American missions. This intercultural exchange has proven beneficial for the whole community, which is now governed as two autonomous provinces within one congregation.

Three

LEADERS IN EDUCATION

The history of education in the United States cannot be fully realized without recognizing the immense contributions of women religious. In 1965, there were over 180,000 women religious in the country, and many of these women were educators.

Following in the footsteps of St. Elizabeth Ann Seton, the Sisters of Charity of Seton Hill focused much of their ministry on education. "The special purpose of the Congregation is the Christian education of youth," the Constitutions of the Sisters of Charity of Seton Hill reflect.

The story begins in 1870 when the Sisters of Charity arrived in Altoona to teach at St. John's parish school. The community gradually expanded to include over 100 schools in the dioceses of Altoona-Johnstown, Greensburg, Pittsburgh, Phoenix, Tucson, Baltimore, Los Angeles, and Washington, DC, among others.

In addition to Catholic parochial schools throughout the United States and two early flagship schools in Greensburg, the community founded the first Montessori School in Westmoreland County, Elizabeth Seton High School in Pittsburgh, and one of the first Catholic colleges for women in Western Pennsylvania.

The sisters entered the field of special education in 1908 with the opening of DePaul Institute, a joint collaboration school with the Diocese of Pittsburgh, for deaf and hard of hearing children. Seton Hill College, founded in 1918 by the Sisters of Charity, transformed into a nationally recognized Catholic liberal arts coeducational university.

The Sisters of Charity of Seton Hill are leaders in the field of education, having served as principals, directors of religious education, teachers, consultants, superintendents, deans, and college presidents.

Generations of Western Pennsylvanians speak to the positive influence of their "angels"—the teachers in black cap and dress, later wearing a ring and necklace as their insignia, who taught them lessons, prepared them for the world, and showed them a glimpse of God.

Sacred Heart Elementary School in the East Liberty neighborhood was among the first missions of the Sisters of Charity in the Diocese of Pittsburgh. When they arrived in 1875, they conducted the parochial school, as well as a paid academy. In the early 1890s, Sr. Mary Grace Ryan (fourth from left) and Sr. M. Basilia Cronin (sixth from left) were given charge of the school choir.

This group of sisters stationed at Sacred Heart Elementary School in the early 1900s poses behind Sacred Heart Church in Pittsburgh. Included in this photograph are, from left to right, (sitting, top to bottom) Canice Holohan, Georgianna Streiff, Eveline Fisher, Eugene Farley, Berenice Conners, Mary Grace Ryan, and Maria Benedict Monahan; (standing) Srs. Claudia Glenn, Francis Regis Enright, Regis Doran, Adele McCullough, and Marie Bernard Trexler. Three future mother superiors, Glenn, Monahan, and Fisher, are featured in this picture.

Sacred Heart High School, founded in 1913 by the parish pastor, Msgr. Francis Keane, became one of the largest Catholic high schools in the city of Pittsburgh. Pictured is a coeducational class of Sacred Heart students in 1929. Sacred Heart functioned as an all-girls educational facility after 1930, although, the 1940s saw a period of coeducation again at Sacred Heart. In 1989, Sacred Heart merged with St. Paul Cathedral High School to form Oakland Catholic High School.

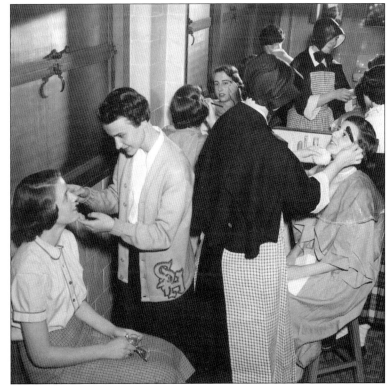

Serving in the roles of principal, teacher, administrator, advisor, and friend, the Sisters of Charity of Seton Hill were the mainstay at Sacred Heart. Former students may recall the many talents of their drama teacher, Sr. Mary Zoe Dorsa. Here, she helps students in the 1950s prepare hair and makeup for the school play.

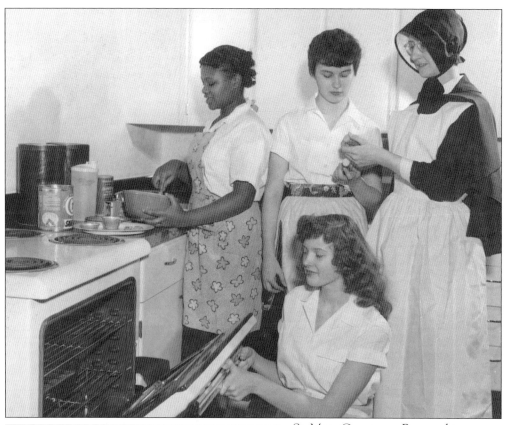

Sr. Mary Constance Rupprecht helped prepare Sacred Heart High School students in home economics. While many young graduates went on to fruitful careers and happy home lives, dozens of women from Sacred Heart entered religious life with the Sisters of Charity of Seton Hill.

The Sisters of Charity of Seton Hill have never been afraid to roll up their sleeves and work hard, but the sisters also know when it is time to play. In this photograph from the 1950s, Sr. Mary Janet Ryan prepares to swing at the annual Sacred Heart High School student-faculty baseball game.

Sisters of Charity of Seton Hill have always been open to new teaching methods and styles. During the 1960s, a team of sister-teachers taught biology. Sr. Alexine Beam at Sacred Heart High School in East Liberty gives a lecture to the entire class using an overhead projector with slides of her own design.

St. John the Evangelist parish, one of the oldest of the Diocese of Pittsburgh, invited the Sisters of Charity to teach at the well-established and wealthy school in 1876. A decade later, Srs. Ernestine Gority and Patrice McGuire founded the first surplice choir in the diocese at St. John's. Note Sr. Isabel Murray posing with this parish class from 1896.

Srs. Mary John Minehan (left) and Gertrude McCarthy (right) pose with the St. John the Baptist School class of 1948 in Pittsburgh, Pennsylvania. Father Wigley is seen at center. The sisters came to St. John's parish in 1879 and taught at both the elementary school and the all-girls high school, which was opened in 1924 and later merged with St. Augustine High School to form Lawrenceville Catholic in 1968.

One week after the sisters arrived in Greensburg in 1882, Fr. Athanasius Hintenach, Order of St. Benedict (OSB), pastor of the Most Holy Sacrament Church, asked the sisters to staff St. Benedict School. At the time, it was a German-speaking parish, and the sisters nicknamed it "the German school." By 1951, it was known as Blessed Sacrament Cathedral School. Sr. Rita Vincent Henderson engages with students at the Blessed Sacrament Cathedral School library in 1973.

Fr. Michael Murphy opened Immaculate Conception School in Irwin in 1878 with a team of lay staff. After the sisters moved to Greensburg in 1882, Father Murphy recruited them to operate the parish school. Immaculate Conception parish fully supported the school into the 1940s, providing new boards, desks, and free books as the population increased. This photograph from 1947 features the choir boys with their teachers Srs. Annina Fox (left) and Mildred Corvi (right).

In 2018, the Sisters of Charity of Seton Hill bade a final farewell to St. Philip's School in Crafton, Pennsylvania, after 133 years in the parish, when Sr. Geraldine Marr retired as principal. The sisters administered the school from 1885 until 1891, when it closed. They returned in 1915 at the request of Fr. William Kelty. In this class photograph from 1935, Srs. Miriam Fidelis Guinagh (left) and Demetria McMahon (right) pose with their students.

The sisters went to St. James's parish in 1886 to begin a new school in Wilkinsburg. Sr. Agnes Marie Reuber (left), with the class of 1921, was one of more than 22 Sister of Charity principals at St. James School. Sr. Marie Margaret Wolf was the last sister-principal of the school in 2013 after the school had merged to become Sr. Thea Bowman Catholic Academy.

Founded in 1883, Holy Cross Church in the South Side of Pittsburgh grew to serve the steel mill families of the local Jones and Laughlin steel mill. The neighborhood grew to include dozens of row homes full of Irish Catholics and Eastern European immigrants. The Sisters of Charity served the parish school faithfully until the parish and all of the homes were razed to build an expanded mill, called the South Side Works, in 1950. Pictured is the neighborhood with portions of the school, rectory, church, and convent visible in the late 1940s.

Pictured with her eighth grade students from Holy Cross School in 1906, Sr. Stanislaus McVay, a graduate of St. Joseph's Academy, would go on to become a history professor and administrator at Seton Hill College.

At the request of Rev. Thomas Briley, the sisters staffed St. Kieran's parish school in Lawrenceville beginning in 1888. In this photograph from 1911 are, from left to right, Srs. Ambrose Timon, Hilary Reilly, Regis Doran, and Agatha Kaney with three young well-dressed students from St. Kieran's at Kennywood Park.

St. John the Baptist School in Scottdale, Pennsylvania, was founded by Rev. M.A. Lambing in 1889. Lambing sought only the best for his parish. This photograph of the sister-teachers at St. John the Baptist shows the great confidence and fortitude of, from left to right, (first row) Srs. Mary Xavier Farrell, Elizabeth McGurgan, Anna Marie Furlong, and Margaret Mary McNamara, (second row) Srs. Anselm Kinane, M. Regis Doran, and Margaret Cecelia Brennan.

Shown are the rectory, church, and school of St. John the Baptist parish in Scottdale, Pennsylvania, before razing for new builds in 1978. The Sisters of Charity served at St. John's for nearly a century. Scottdale, a town at the center of the coal and coke industry in the late 19th and early 20th centuries, would find itself struggling after the Depression. The school closed for several years before reopening in 1941.

After Fr. Daniel Devlin invited the Sisters of Charity to St. Stephen's School in Hazelwood in 1892, the school became one of the largest Sisters of Charity schools in Western Pennsylvania. Over 200 women religious helped shape the history of St. Stephen's. Pictured around 1918 is Sr. Geraldine Fardy, principal, with students of St. Stephen's School.

St. Luke's Roman Catholic parish was established in the borough of Mansfield, which later became known as Carnegie, near Pittsburgh, in 1867. Fr. Patrick J. Quilter welcomed the Sisters of Charity to the parish school in 1899. Pictured is St. Luke's Church from that same year. The parish would merge with several others in 1992 to form St. Elizabeth Ann Seton Church, named as such due to the connection with the sisters' foundress.

The growth of industry in the neighborhood of Carnegie prompted an expansion of the church and school. In fact, a coeducational high school was added to the already flourishing parish grade school in 1927. Sr. Teresa Clare Kernan (center) served as principal of St. Luke's High School in 1941.

Homestead, Pennsylvania, a bustling steel mill neighborhood best known for the infamous strike of 1892, was home to throngs of first- and second-generation immigrant Catholics. Six Catholic schools within the district catered to poor and middle-class students of different ethnic backgrounds. An impressively dressed group of young graduates from St. Mary Magdalene's School in 1909 poses with Sr. M. Borgia Casey. Perhaps, these same students would witness the great decline of Homestead after the collapse of the steel industry.

1909

When Holy Innocents parish was established in the Sheraden neighborhood of Pittsburgh in 1900, the sisters at Seton Hill were placed in charge of religious education. It was not until the school building was completed in 1908 that they also took charge of the school. Anticipating a school with six grades, Fr. Daniel O'Shea asked for six sisters, but the parishioners begged for a seventh grade, so another teacher was quickly recruited to accommodate the parish's growing needs.

Bishop Regis Canevin founded the Pittsburgh School for the Deaf in the Lappe mansion on Lowrie Street in the Troy Hill neighborhood of Pittsburgh in 1908. There was a great need in the city for an educational facility for Catholic deaf students who desired a religious education. Three Sisters of Charity of Seton Hill were immediately sent to the Boston School for the Deaf for training. The school opened with one student.

Student enrollment increased quickly, and the Pittsburgh School for the Deaf became known as DePaul Institute. This photograph shows Srs. Martha Walsh (second row, fourth from left) and Marie Antonia McLinden (second row, second from right) with students in 1910. Sr. Marie Antonia spent nearly 50 years as teacher, administrator, and principal at DePaul Institute. Her legacy at DePaul has been felt by generations of alumni.

DePaul Institute emphasized oral-aural training of the hearing-impaired. By developing auditory skills, lipreading, and articulation, students were encouraged to improve their own expressive speech. Sign language was not part of the curriculum. This photograph shows a young student, Sandy, learning how to pronounce the word "doll" with the help of Sr. Bridgetta Fitzpatrick.

The sisters at DePaul Institute began incorporating blind curriculum into deaf education in 1948. Sr. Francis Louise Honeychuck, seen here with students in 1955, earned blind education certification by transcribing the children's book *Black Beauty* into braille. She advocated for accommodations in the classroom and, with Sr. Angelica Little, created *Talking Prayer Book for the Blind*. The sisters offered classes to the visually impaired until 1970.

By 1910, DePaul Institute had relocated to Mount Lebanon and the expanding student body prompted Fr. Raymond Doherty to construct a new building in 1949. He named it Our Lady of Victory Hall. When Sr. Marie Antonia studied deaf education in Massachusetts, she visited the Shrine of Our Lady of Victory in Lackawanna, New York. She instilled a devotion to Our Lady in the pupils of DePaul Institute, which continued for many years.

At DePaul Institute, the sisters assigned to work with deaf and hard of hearing children utilized the latest techniques and technological advancements in deaf education. In this photograph from the late 1940s, Sr. Bridgetta Fitzpatrick utilizes a microphone and headsets to recite the Pledge of Allegiance with two young students.

The sisters at DePaul Institute encouraged students to pursue extracurricular activities. From a very early period, each DePaul student was required to join the Boy Scouts or Girl Scouts, even the preschoolers had an "unofficial" scouting program called Peeps and Playmates. Here, Sr. Florita McGrory is presenting the Ad Virginem Award to the Girl Scouts at DePaul in the 1950s.

The Sisters of Charity went to St. Anselm's parish in the Swissvale neighborhood of Pittsburgh in 1910 to staff the elementary school. The immense success of Westinghouse Electric and the Union Signal and Switch industrial plants led to a population explosion in Swissvale in the early years. By 1955, Rev. Clarence Sanderbeck, recognizing the need for a high school, asked the Sisters of Charity for help. They opened St. Anselm's in September 1957. Unfortunately, enrollment declined in the 1970s, and the school closed in 1978.

One of nearly 300 Sisters of Charity missioned to St. Anselm's, Sr. M. Antoinette Bosco checks the bus list before the 1960s elementary students depart for Storybook Forest at Idlewild Park in Ligonier, Pennsylvania. The year 1960 saw a peak enrollment of 1,300 students at St. Anselm's, from kindergarten through eighth grade.

These children at St. John Gualbert School in Johnstown, Pennsylvania, do not yet know what they will have to endure. Three years prior to the deadly, devastating Johnstown Flood of 1889, Sr. Mary Regina Fitzmaurice (back, center) and Fr. T. Rosensteel (left) pose with their class. The Sisters of Charity survived the flood but would not return to St. John's after that historic event.

The first sisters to return to Johnstown, Pennsylvania, after the devastating flood of May 1889 were, from left to right, (sitting) Srs. Mechtildes Grasberger, Liguori Gillespie, Agnes Francina Kearney, and Margaret McMahon; (standing) Agnes Cecelia Dougherty, Alacoque McHale, and Irene Taylor. They taught at St. Columba's School in Johnstown, which had been damaged, but not destroyed, in the flood. The sisters' tenure at St. Columba's lasted until 1905.

In 1912, Resurrection School in the Brookline neighborhood of Pittsburgh began an elementary school and a two-year commercial school in place of traditional high school. Five Sisters of Charity conducted the school with Sr. Mary Helena Degnan as principal of the elementary school and Mother Mary Joseph Havey as principal of the commercial school. Pictured here in the 1940s is Sr. Ida Marie McCarthy with elementary students. Two future Sisters of Charity, Srs. Barbara Ann Boss and Patricia Laffey, stand in the second row from the top.

Growth within the neighborhood of Brookline led to increased enrollment at Resurrection School through the 1940s and 1950s, reaching a peak of 2,000 students by 1961. Sr. M. Cecelia Ward, diocesan music supervisor, teaches a group of Resurrection girls in school uniforms how to play the harpsichord in the mid-1960s.

Sr. Mary Coleman Kilkeary, who entered the community in 1934, taught at Resurrection School from 1961 until 1967. Known as an extraordinary teacher, Sr. Mary Coleman quizzes her students in reading at Resurrection School in this photograph. Sr. Mary Coleman lived to be 100 and died in 2018.

This photograph shows Sr. M. Francesca Brownlee (left) with St. Joseph's Academy student Mayme Quinn and Sr. Anita McGinnis in the art studio around 1910. The students and graduates of St. Joseph's Academy began clamoring for coursework beyond the high school level. In 1914, Clara McCormick expressed interest in college courses, so Mother Mary Francis McCullough approved the foundation of a junior college.

The Seton Junior College grew but could not flourish without accreditation and expansion. Sr. M. Francesca Brownlee, with her colleague Sr. Clementine Oler, traveled to Harrisburg in 1917 to pursue an official charter for a Catholic women's college. The College and University Council of Pennsylvania reviewed the college but determined it lacked an endowment and needed improvements in the science laboratories and the library. Seen here in 1922 is the college library established by generous benefactors. Also shown is the physics laboratory funded by the families of the sisters. With these improvements, the sisters were able to argue that the sum of their real estate holdings, as well as the lives of the sisters, would serve as an endowment for the college. On June 3, 1918, the sisters received their official charter for Seton Hill College and were able to confer degrees in art, music, and home economics.

Seton Hill College students, from left to right, (first row) Mary Boggs, Margaret Garrity, and Mary O'Toole, (second row) Rose Irene Boggs, Mayme D'Amico, Marian Mohan, Agnes Farabaugh, and Grace Kaplan pose in front of the Administration Building in the early 1920s. After earning her degree in Latin, Rose Irene Boggs entered the Sisters of Charity in 1931 and became the registrar of Seton Hill College from 1948 until 1971.

This c. 1957 aerial view of the Seton Hill College campus shows the growth of the campus in less than 50 years. Additions to the Administration Building and Chapel Annex included Canevin Hall, Lowe Hall, St. Joseph Hall, and Maura Hall. In this photograph, Sullivan Hall, the Faculty/Priest House, Reeves Library, and Havey Hall can also be seen. In the distance, the sisters' cemetery and St. Philomena Shrine are visible, as well as Maryglen Cabin.

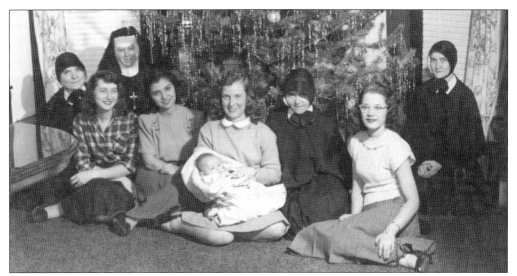

Home economics majors of the college may remember the "practice house" at St. Mary's, the former Stokes mansion. Young women learned proper home management, and an orphaned baby from Roselia was temporarily "adopted" and cared for by students. The babies were then picked up by their new parents at Seton Hill. This Christmas photograph from the mid-1940s shows Srs. Rose Marie Schneider (left), Rose Angela Cunningham (center), and Alphonse Griffin (right) with an unidentified Felician sister and home economics students.

Over the years, degree programs at Seton Hill College expanded to include the sciences, mathematics, liberal arts programs, and much more. This undated image from the science laboratory shows Sr. Germaine Helwig (second from right) demonstrating biology with animal specimens to, from left to right, Srs. Edith Marie Fullen, Mary Peter Murphy, Jude Thaddeus O'Donnell, and Vivian Walch. Many of the sisters also earned their undergraduate degrees from Seton Hill College by taking Saturday courses while on mission.

The Catholic identity of Seton Hill College has always been at the forefront of the curriculum and student life. In 1914, the St. Joseph's Academy Alumnae Association funded the building of the Grotto of Our Lady of Lourdes to serve the students of the three Seton Hill Schools (St. Mary's School for Boys, St. Joseph's Academy, and Seton Hill College). This photograph from the 1950s shows three college students conducting a ceremony at the shrine.

A lush, springtime scene shows Seton Hill College students enjoying a moment on the swings between Maura Hall and the Administration Building, showcasing the Chapel Annex rose window, in the 1940s. The natural beauty and old-world architecture of the campus has attracted generations of students to Seton Hill.

Beginning in 1939, Sr. Miriam Joseph Murphy, known as "Mimi Jo" to her students, began working in the English department of Seton Hill College. She particularly loved teaching Shakespeare. Sr. Miriam Joseph was often more than a professor to students; she became a friend, confidante, and ardent supporter. In fact, she mentored and befriended a young Joanne Woodyard, who later become Dr. Joanne Woodyard Boyle, president of Seton Hill College from 1987 until 2013.

Seton Hill College has had a stellar music program forged from the legacy of the very first sister-musicians in the 1890s who hosted a separate music school from the academy. Here, Sr. Helen Muha, chairwoman of the music department, teaches, from left to right, students Tim Dahlem, Joette Salandro, and Linda Sickler in the music studio. Sister Helen inspired many students to become professional musicians.

The outcomes of Vatican II became more apparent on the Seton Hill campus in the late 1960s. Simultaneous with societal changes, the Sisters of Charity of Seton Hill were making adjustments to their way of life. Sr. Mary Janet Ryan (center), professor of history, and Sr. Colette Toler (right), professor of English, wear their modified habits while working with student Jane McMahon.

A 1957 Seton Hill College yearbook photograph sums up the great influence of the Sisters of Charity in the educational progress, spiritual development, and life of the student. Sr. Helen Elizabeth McElwain stands with a student awaiting graduation ceremonies in St. Joseph Chapel. The Setonian influence persists in the life of all Seton Hill graduates. The sisters still maintain a persistent and influential, albeit smaller, presence on the Seton Hill University campus.

Bishop McCort High School in Johnstown, Pennsylvania, was founded in 1922 as Johnstown Catholic High School. Priests and seven women religious communities were present on the staff. Sr. Frances Holland (left), pictured with her Spanish students in 1967, taught at the school for 14 years.

Altoona Catholic High School, founded in 1922, became Bishop Guilfoyle High School in 1961. In the early 1980s, Sr. Felicita Diggin (seated center) connected with students at Bishop Guilfoyle. Graduates may also remember the great contributions of the sister-sisters, Srs. Cornelia and Clementine O'Friel, natives of Altoona.

The sisters were requested for the new school in Our Lady of Mercy parish in Prospect, Pennsylvania, in 1923. The school began with six grades and expanded to eight grades after the first year. Sr. Frances Holland, seen with Our Lady of Mercy students in 1950, taught at the school for many years.

Another parochial school of the sisters in Altoona was St. Leo's School, which was founded in 1925. This photograph from 1957 shows a proud Sr. Rita Catherine Cole, principal of St. Leo's, with Fr. John P. Manning and Patricia Dyczko, who won a national scholarship in an essay contest, "Why a Catholic Education is Important to Me." She received $500.

Lack of a Catholic high school in the South Hills of Pittsburgh prompted Mother Claudia Glenn to seek a school site for graduates of the eight-grade Resurrection School and other local Catholic students. In 1940, the old West Liberty Grade School on Pioneer Avenue in Brookline became available. Sr. Regina Clare Breig would open the all-girls preparatory Elizabeth Seton High School as principal in September 1941 with 77 students.

Within five years of opening, the student population of Elizabeth Seton High School increased to nearly 400. The "Little Red School on Capital Hill" offered full and rigorous academic programs with engaging extracurricular activities. In this 1947 May Day photograph, the Elizabeth Seton classes of 1949 and 1950 pose around Mary's Quadrangle, erected in honor of the principalship of Sr. Regina Clare Breig.

During the 1960s, a highlight of the sophomore biology class at Elizabeth Seton High School was the dissection of a frog. Sr. Mary Clement (Jane) McNulty assists students of Elizabeth Seton High School during this project, pointing out important points of anatomy.

Graduates of Elizabeth Seton High School could not forget the mechanical talents, kind demeanor, and beautiful tenor tones of the school custodian, Anthony O'Toole, as he maintained the school. O'Toole served tirelessly as the custodian from 1942 until his retirement in 1970. Here, Sr. Mary Jean Petrarca is consulting with students while Anthony O'Toole moves a desk in the late 1960s.

First Communion for young Roman Catholic girls and boys is an important family tradition and a rite of passage among parishioners. These young students from Holy Rosary School in Juniata, Pennsylvania, in 1956 would look to Msgr. Francis McNelis (left), pastor, and Sr. Mary Catherine Coughenour (right) for spiritual guidance in the months leading up to the formal ceremony.

Sr. Harold Ann Jones, principal of St. Bruno School in Greensburg, admires the gift of a television set from Davis's Food Market in 1961. Sr. Harold Ann Jones was principal of the school from 1956 until 1963.

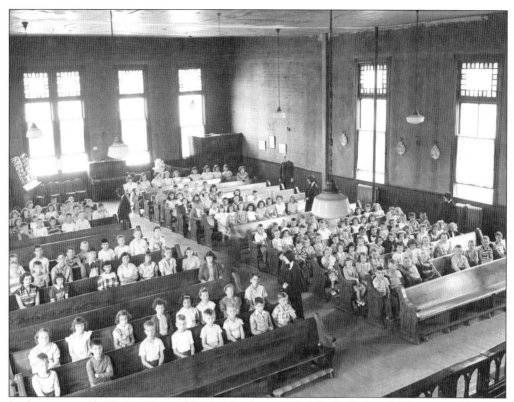

In the summer of 1951, Srs. Ermanilda Knepley, Lucia Wilt, Elizabeth Ann Mahoney, and Reynita Flynn taught vacation classes at St. James parish in Apollo. Fr. James O'Hanlon is visible in the rear of the photograph. The sisters were recruited to staff the new parish school in 1955.

In 1953, Srs. Ida Marie McCarthy, Teresina Bridges, and Grace Marie Hurd (shown from left to right) arrived at a century-old farmhouse in Bethesda, Maryland, to open St. Jane de Chantal Elementary School. Pictured is that first group of sisters with their class of students and parish pastor, Msgr. James Caulfield. The sisters withdrew from the school in 1995 but not before leaving an indelible impression on the people of the Archdiocese of Washington, DC.

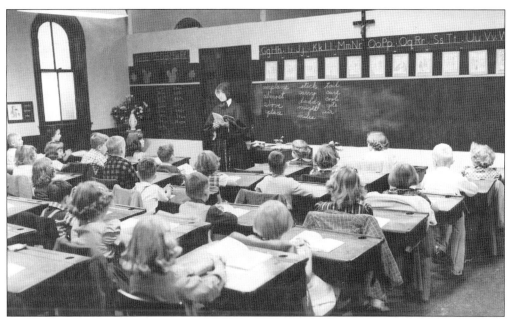

Sr. M. Ellenita O'Connor, pictured teaching second and third grade, was among the first five sisters missioned to St. Jerome School in Charleroi, Pennsylvania, in 1953. She stayed at St. Jerome until 1956. Sr. Marie Cecily Chartener served as principal while Sr. Mary Kevin Kerrigan, Anna Marie Miller, and Mary Mildred Nolan also served that first school year.

In 1956, the Sisters of Charity expanded their missions in Maryland to include Sacred Heart School in Glyndon. A total of 59 sisters served as principals and teachers at Sacred Heart until 1984, when the community withdrew. In this c. 1967 photograph, Srs. Marie Dominic Reese (left) and Mary Ellen Jeffreys (center) with an unidentified Sister of Christian Charity engage students in a folk song.

A Sister of Charity reviews a student publication with a group of students at Bishop Boyle High School in 1963. The school was named after Bishop Hugh Charles Boyle, who served as Pittsburgh's sixth bishop from 1921 until 1950. Bishop Boyle opened in 1962 in the renovated St. Mary Magdalen School building in Homestead but closed in 1987.

"How are our fish doing? Do I get to take them home on holiday?" "I will take good care of them." Former sister Paul Francis (Georgeanne) Halchak assures her students at St. Therese Elementary School in Munhall that the fish are thriving. The school was started in 1954 with Sr. Mary Clifford Soisson as the founding principal. The school is thriving at this time.

Pittsburgh native Fr. Joseph Lucey was appointed to Our Lady of Lourdes parish in Abbeville, Louisiana, in 1953. The African American parish school, established by St. Katherine Drexel in 1925, had fallen into hard times. Father Lucey sought experienced teachers. Mother Claudia sent, from left to right, Srs. Raymond Fatora, Teresina Bridges, and Elizabeth Ann Stock to Abbeville in 1956. A fire at Our Lady of Lourdes Church and local issues with Catholic school integration prompted the sisters to withdraw from the school in 1973.

Sr. Mary Michael Burns spent several years in the early 1970s at Our Lady of Lourdes in Abbeville, Louisiana. The black community of Abbeville was grateful to the sisters for nearly 20 years of dedicated service while the sisters were equally appreciative to the community for gracious hospitality. Pictured is Sr. Mary Michael with her Dominic Salvio Club members.

Greensburg Central Catholic School opened in September 1959. A number of religious communities were represented on the staff of this Westmoreland County school. Initially, the Sisters of Charity were placed in charge of the science and music departments by Supt. Rev. Harry G. Hynes. Later, they would hold the principalship, among other teaching positions.

From left to right, Srs. Ida Marie McCarthy, Mary Halloran, and Kevin Mary Mannion were the first three sisters missioned to Mother of Sorrows School in Murrysville, Pennsylvania, in 1962. Here, they are pictured with their students and Fr. Regis Hickey, pastor of Mother of Sorrows parish.

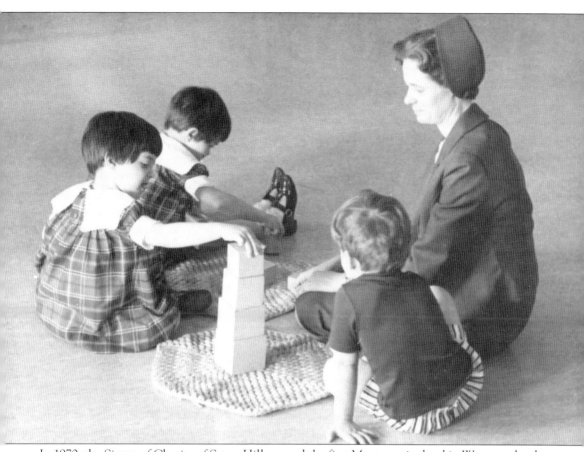

In 1970, the Sisters of Charity of Seton Hill opened the first Montessori school in Westmoreland County under the leadership of Sr. Anita Schulte, a woman following the visionary teachings of both Elizabeth Ann Seton and Maria Montessori. Here, she is pictured with the first students, Florence and Lucy Lonigro and Christian Davis. The school now functions independently as Elizabeth Seton Montessori School on Frye Farm Road in Greensburg.

Sr. Kathyrn Palas sets up a microscope for two students at Seton-LaSalle High School in Mount Lebanon, Pennsylvania, in 1995. The Sisters of Charity's all-girls Elizabeth Seton High School merged with the all-boys South Hills Catholic High School in 1979 to form Seton-LaSalle. The sisters have maintained a presence on the campus in the ensuing years.

Conn-Area Catholic School, formed out of a consolidation of parochial primary schools in Fayette County, appealed to the Sisters of Charity at the urging of Bishop William Connare in 1984. They needed a principal. Sr. Brycelyn Eyler was the first Sister of Charity principal. Pictured is Sr. Eileen Johnstown, a later principal of Conn-Area Catholic, reading with students in the school library in 1995. At Conn-Area Catholic, Srs. Catherine Meinert and Beatrice Ann Parenti implemented one of the first parochial after-school extended-care programs in the region in 1996.

Four

HEALTH CARE
AND HEALING

A baby left on a convent doorstep on March 17, 1884, began the quest for the Sisters of Charity to establish their first health-care institution, a medical facility and orphanage for foundlings and unwed mothers. With the help of Roselia and Charles Donnelly and other benefactors, the sisters opened a small house in July 1891. By the end of the first month, the admission of 19 infants stressed the limits of the building. The need for additional space prompted Charles Donnelly to purchase the old Ursuline Academy in the Hill District of Pittsburgh. It became known as Roselia Foundling and Maternity Asylum.

As the need for health care in the eastern suburbs of Pittsburgh grew, the Sisters of Charity responded to the request of physicians to administer Charity Hospital. Three sisters, without professional training, courageously took responsibility for a nine-room hospital in February 1897, which grew to a 22-bed hospital by April. By December 1905, the hospital, by then known as Pittsburgh Hospital, found a permanent home on the former Finley property on Frankstown Avenue. Pittsburgh Hospital School of Nursing was established that same year and graduated the first class with five Sisters of Charity and five young laywomen in the spring of 1908.

From this small beginning, the health-care ministry spread, and Sister of Charity nurses could be found in hospitals, nursing facilities, and clinics throughout Western Pennsylvania. Over 160 sisters in the community would switch from black cap and habit to the white cap for service in health care.

Providence Hospital and School of Nursing in Beaver Falls, Pennsylvania, became a ministry in 1909. Later, Mother Claudia Glenn teamed with the Diocese of Greensburg to fill the need for a quality health-care facility in the city of Jeannette, near Greensburg. After more than a decade of fundraising, Jeannette District Memorial Hospital was opened in 1958.

As health care needs changed, the Sisters of Charity were active members of the American Health and Catholic Health Organizations and professional nursing organizations. They became advocates of better salaries and shorter workweeks and days. Their concern for the sick, forgotten, and outcast spread to home and hospice nursing, nursing education, and continuing care for the elderly.

The sisters began conducting Roselia Foundling and Maternity Hospital in the city of Pittsburgh in July 1891. Charles Donnelly, a wealthy businessman and financier, and his wife, Mary Roselia, were ardent supporters of the cause. They purchased the former Ursuline Academy on Cliff and Manilla Streets for use as a permanent home for foundlings. Roselia died around this time, and the hospital was named for her.

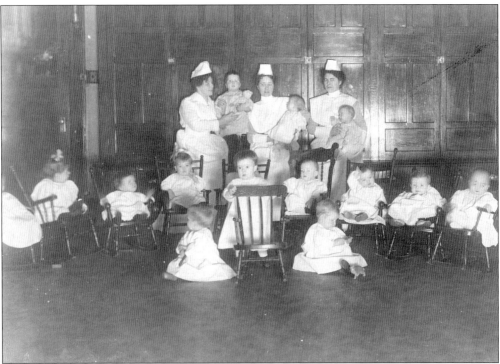

The original Roselia Foundling building included a "waif's basket," a revolving deposit box where babies could be abandoned but kept warm inside. Unwed pregnant women were also offered adequate maternity care and counseling. In later years, a pregnant woman might spend weeks or months in the hospital before delivering her child. Pictured are three lay nurses with more than a dozen foundling children at Roselia.

On Christmas Eve 1928, an infant girl was abandoned at the Sheridan Theater in Pittsburgh. She was found by the theater manager and a young future dancer and film star, Gene Kelly. The girl was placed into the care of the sisters at Roselia. The theater owner's theatrical social club, the Variety Club, decided to "adopt" her by giving financial support. This tradition continued every year through Roselia, and each baby was named Catherine "Variety" Sheridan. The Variety Club attracted wealthy and influential men in Hollywood and film, including Perry Como. The organization is now known as Variety International Children's Fund and donates millions of dollars to children in need across the globe. Pictured is one Catherine Sheridan receiving gifts from Variety members in 1952. In the photograph below, the 1952 Variety Club Telethon included Perry Como (right) as a performer.

The Variety Club of Pittsburgh funded the building of a new facility for Roselia Foundling and Maternity Hospital in 1956. It was named Philip Murray Memorial Hall. At that time, the deed to the property was gifted to the Sisters of Charity by the Variety Club. The new building appears in this 1956 photograph. Here, Srs. James Regis Stewart (center, in black) and Mary Bede McLaughlin (right) play with the "run-arounds."

From 1891 until 1971, over 27,000 orphaned and temporarily boarded children came through Roselia. This number does not include the thousands of women who opted to deliver their babies through the maternity wing. This image from 1954 shows a sister engaging children in the playroom of the old Roselia building on Cliff and Manila Streets.

Sr. Raphael Kane entered the Sisters of Charity in 1877. Her influence helped to secure benefactors for the Roselia Foundling and Maternity Hospital in 1891. She led Srs. Vincent Finnegan and Serena Grady as the first administrator of Charity Hospital in Pittsburgh. A team of doctors founded the hospital on Stanton Avenue in 1897. The Sisters of Charity joined the staff shortly thereafter and went on to fully govern the facility.

This picture of Mrs. John McClory and her son is dated 1894. Mrs. McClory was the first patient of Charity Hospital. The hospital, a nine-room house, became crowded and moved to a duplex at Collins Avenue and Hoeveler Street in Pittsburgh in April 1897. Charity Hospital received its formal charter on January 14, 1898.

The sisters purchased the Finley estate, bordered by Frankstown Avenue, Washington Boulevard, and Shetland and Finley Streets, in 1902 to accommodate the growing hospital. The residence there served as the hospital until 1904, when the permanent structure was completed. The home was then used as the nurses' residence. Locals commonly called the facility Pittsburgh Hospital, so the name was officially changed from Charity to Pittsburgh Hospital in 1908.

Here is a view of Pittsburgh Hospital from Washington Boulevard. Silver Lake can be seen. The first floor of the hospital had an emergency room and business offices while the second, third, and fourth floors housed patient units. The operating suites were situated on the top floor.

The original operating room in Pittsburgh Hospital was completed in 1904 and utilized until the late 1960s. In 1908, the operating room served as the venue for the graduation ceremony for Pittsburgh Hospital School of Nursing's first graduating class, which consisted of 10 students. Sr. Irenaeus Joyce, a member of the class, remarked, "It was the only room large enough to house a graduation."

This formal picture shows, from left to right, (first row) Srs. Marie Fidelis Bridge, Luigi Walsh, and Irenaeus Joyce; (second row) Srs. Marcella Renninger and Isadore Boyce, the first five Sister of Charity graduates from the Pittsburgh Hospital School of Nursing in 1908. A nurse from Johns Hopkins Hospital in Baltimore directed the program. Following graduation, three sisters joined the hospital staff. Sister Irenaeus became administrator of Providence Hospital in Beaver Falls. Sister Marcella became director of the nursing school.

Sr. Marcella Renninger poses with the starched and proper members of the Pittsburgh Hospital graduating class of 1913. One young woman (first row, fourth from left) entered the Sisters of Charity that same year. Mary Hartnett, known by the religious name of Sr. M. Rita, became administrator of the Pittsburgh Hospital.

Up until the mid-1940s, sheep could often be seen grazing on the grounds of Pittsburgh Hospital. The sheep were utilized by laboratory technicians for testing. This area of property would become the site for the nurses' residence, erected in 1946.

Sr. Vincent McDermott broke ground for the new nurses' residence at Pittsburgh Hospital School of Nursing on August 29, 1945. Two members of the first graduating class, Srs. Marcella Renninger (left) and Irenaeus Joyce (right), join Sr. Rita Hartnett (center), administrator, for the celebration. The building was partially completed and occupied in 1947 and fully occupied with a capacity for 175 students in 1948.

Sr. Paul Gabriel Wilhere served at Pittsburgh Hospital as the director of nursing education from 1947 until 1955. She returned to work as the in-service coordinator and the emergency room supervisor in the 1960s. She became a consultant for the Pennsylvania Health Department and the Department of Welfare, in addition to teaching at Penn State University, the University of Pittsburgh, and Catholic University of America.

Sr. Rita Hartnett (center), administrator of Pittsburgh Hospital, joins the nurses and child patients to pass out some Christmas stockings and bring a little cheer during the 1952 holiday season. Sister Rita encouraged decorations to keep the spirit of the season alive.

Sr. Irenaeus Joyce, a visionary administrator of Providence Hospital, initiated a hospital-based prepayment plan to assure hospital care in the area during the Great Depression. She charged 50¢ per month to subscribers and enrolled several thousand. It was a health insurance prototype. When the Hospital Service Association conceived an insurance plan, the precursor to Blue Cross, Sister Irenaeus placed her thriving fund into the plan in 1935.

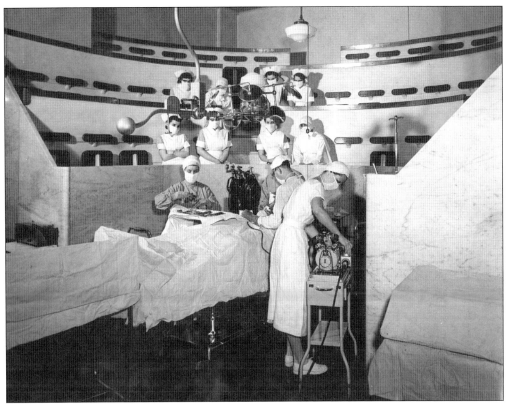

Students from the Pittsburgh Hospital class of 1955 observe surgery in the large, original operating room that was built in 1908. The surgeon and scrub nurse are unidentified. George Tegzes, anesthesiologist, is at the head of the patient. Harriet Phillips, RN, is the circulating nurse.

The capping ceremony for the Pittsburgh Hospital School of Nursing class of 1955 took place in the Stephen Foster Memorial Auditorium at the University of Pittsburgh. Sr. Paul Gabriel Wilhere announces the names of graduates as Sr. Miriam Francis Cunningham and Patricia Scuffle, RN, cap the students. William Gibson, MD, and an unidentified priest sit on the left of the stage. A senior student portraying Florence Nightingale lights the nursing candle for each student.

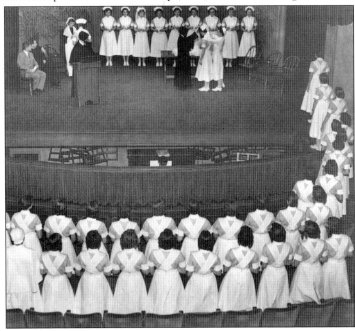

Sr. Mary Ida Gannon opens the door of the final wing of Pittsburgh Hospital in 1963. Sr. Mary Ida joined the staff in 1928 and served as financial officer for many years. With the retirement of Sr. Rita Hartnett, Sr. Mary Ida became administrator. Known for her compassion and quick wit, she initiated many innovative changes and greater outreach to the local community.

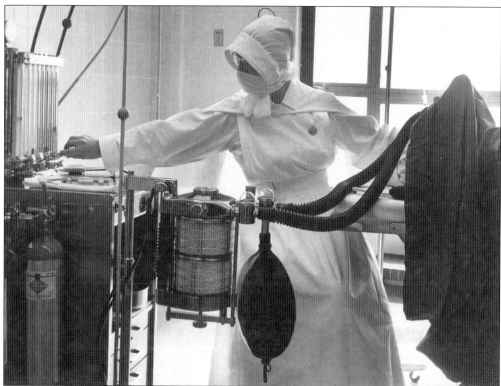

Sr. Marion Bianco, nurse anesthetist, assists with surgery in one of the newly completed operating rooms in the 1963 wing of Pittsburgh Hospital. Sister Marion graduated from the School of Nursing in 1955. She then attended the anesthesia school, which George Tegzes, anesthesiologist, conducted at the hospital.

Three nurses and an unidentified Sister of Charity prepare meals in the kitchen of Providence Hospital in the 1900s. The uniforms and caps would suggest that the young women are nurses, perhaps student nurses. At the request of Fr. J.M. Wertz, Providence Hospital opened in 1909, after the sisters purchased the Reeves mansion property in Beaver Falls, Pennsylvania. It was the second general hospital of the Sisters of Charity. In the undated picture below, the Reeves mansion is visible on the right with the first hospital wing on the left. Sr. DePaul Brennan was appointed superintendent. Given the grand sum of $10 to convert the mansion to a hospital, Sister DePaul opened the facility with the help of a sister-nurse, a pharmacist, and women from Father Wertz's parish.

During the annual visit of mothers and babies during National Hospital Day, a group of former patients of Providence Hospital poses at the hospital entrance in the 1930s. The practice of inviting mothers and babies back for a yearly visit continued until the hospital merged in 1967.

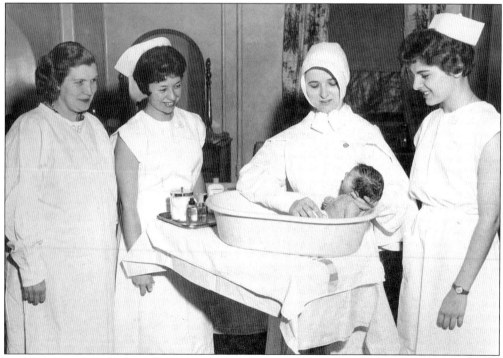

Sr. Marie Agnes (Maureen) Halloran demonstrates the bathing procedure of a newborn for a mother and two Providence Hospital School of Nursing students. Sister Maureen graduated from Providence Hospital School of Nursing in 1957 and served from 1959 until 1963 as the supervisor of the obstetrical floor.

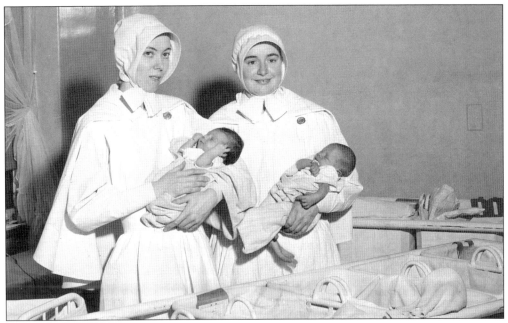

Pictured in the 1950s, Srs. M. Camillus Erb (left) and Grace Hayes (right) hold babies in the nursery of Providence Hospital. Providence Hospital merged with Beaver Valley General Hospital in New Brighton and later with Rochester Hospital to form the Beaver Valley Medical Center. The Sisters of Charity withdrew from the hospital in the spring of 1967.

Sister of Charity nursing staff mentored Providence Hospital nursing students with the latest technology. Seen around 1960 is Sr. Bernardine Lauer with a young student testing the sterilizing machine.

In 1947, Joseph Conomino began a movement for Jeannette District Memorial Hospital, called "Operation Hospital." The City of Jeannette donated 6.5 acres of land, plans were drawn, and a drive for funds began. The funds provided for exterior construction of a 50-bed hospital. In 1952, an additional fundraiser proved inadequate, and construction was halted. By 1955, interested partners revived the movement. The Sisters of Charity teamed with the Diocese of Greensburg to make the hospital come to fruition.

Mother M. Claudia Glenn prepares to speak at the dedication of Jeannette District Memorial Hospital on July 19, 1959, after an introduction by Thomas Curtin, president of the Jeannette Hospital Association Board. Msgr. Cyril Vogel (later Bishop of Selma, Kansas) and Bishop Hugh L. Lamb, first bishop of Greensburg, are honored guests.

It appears that the entire town of Jeannette came out to the dedication of Jeannette District Memorial Hospital in 1959. Local and religious leaders dreamed of this day for over 10 years. The community was just as excited for the event. Over 7,000 people toured the hospital, consuming 21,000 cookies and 285 gallons of punch during the celebration!

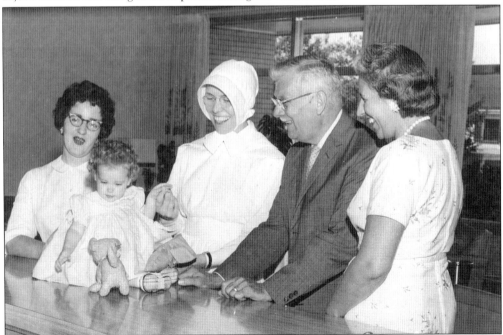

Deborah Jeannette Verelich and her mother celebrate her first birthday under the admiring eyes of, from left to right, Sr. Geraldine Miller, administrator; Carl Sunder, secretary-treasurer of the Board of Trustees; and Lillian Matiska, director of human resources. Deborah was the first baby born in Jeannette District Memorial Hospital on July 29, 1959, only four days after the opening of the facility. The Women's Auxiliary gave her a complete layette set at her birth.

Sr. Mary Magdalen Foley learns to operate the fire extinguishers at Jeannette Hospital during a 1967 in-service day. Fireman Ralph Day conducted the lessons as other employees await their turn. Other sisters shown include Sr. Rose Marie Schneider, an unidentified sister, and Sr. Isabelle Jordan.

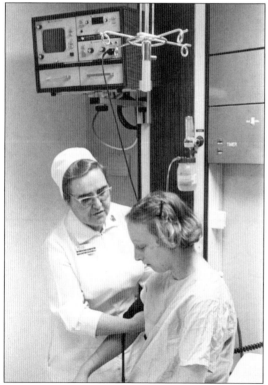

Sr. Mary Bede McLaughlin takes the blood pressure for a young female patient at Jeannette District Memorial Hospital. Sr. Mary Bede McLaughlin graduated from Pittsburgh Hospital School of Nursing in 1946. After entering the community, she ministered as a registered nurse and a supervisor in each of the health-care facilities owned and operated by the Sisters of Charity of Seton Hill.

Five

To Go Where Most Needed

Beyond the missions in schools and hospitals, the Sisters of Charity of Seton Hill have felt called by God to work among the people—all people. This includes those of different faiths, ethnicities, and circumstances. The sisters go where they are called and do what is most needed. The diversified ministries of the Sisters of Charity of Seton Hill range from work among the poor and marginalized to serving as caregivers and spiritual guides to children and adults alike.

The alternative work of the sisters likely began with pastoral ministry. Often, the sisters who served at a parish school would also volunteer time on behalf of the parish in catechetical instruction and social service programs.

Certain missions, like those pursued among the African American community in the Hill District of Pittsburgh, began as proselytizing ventures but turned into vital social service and community programs.

Attending to forgotten and marginalized groups of people, including those in prison, refugees, the elderly, and children, became of deep concern to the Sisters of Charity, particularly within the past 50 years.

Over time, the exceptional talents of certain sisters were fostered in unique ministerial opportunities. For example, creative artistic sisters like Sr. Fides Glass were encouraged to pursue unique projects like illustrating and writing books. Sr. Rosalie O'Hara followed her passion in radio and film education.

This volume could not touch on every instance of unique ministry but will simply highlight a few of the ways in which the Sisters of Charity of Seton Hill have contributed to the good of the world. Feel inspired by these incredible women and reach out a hand to one's neighbor in need.

Sr. Mary Thomas Woods, director of the Free Employment Bureau of Sacred Heart parish, began her ministry on behalf of the poor of Sacred Heart parish in Shadyside, Pittsburgh, in 1934. In addition to securing permanent and temporary work for the unemployed, Sr. Mary Thomas organized donations of clothing, shoes, and food for the poor. In fact, her generosity, particularly around the holidays, earned her the moniker "Sister Santa." This photograph shows Sr. Mary Thomas assisting Santa with donations for poor children in Pittsburgh in the late 1930s.

Sr. Cyril Aaron resigned as dean of women of Seton Hill College in 1942 to pursue work among the African American community in Pittsburgh. She began her ministry by walking the streets of the South Side and the Hill District to converse with the people and discover their needs. Their needs were many and great. With help from the St. Vincent de Paul Society, a redbrick house on Webster Avenue in the Hill District was purchased in 1944. The House of Mary, as it became known, offered social welfare programs, catechetical instruction for children and adults, and community gatherings.

Through the House of Mary, 2,000 black Pittsburghers were welcomed into the Catholic Church. Far more received donations of food, clothing, coal to warm their homes, and community support. By 1962, the House of Mary was exceeding capacity. Bishop John J. Wright of Pittsburgh approved the construction of the Frederic Ozanam School and Cultural Center. In addition to a primary school, preschool, and Montessori school, the center hosted cultural events, adult classes and lectures, and after-school programs. This photograph shows Sr. Rose Elizabeth Breen (left) and Sr. Cyril Aaron (right) with a large class of students at the Frederic Ozanam Center in 1962.

The Ozanam Strings, an award-winning inner-city youth orchestra, began under the guidance of Sr. Francis Assisi Gorham in the Hill District of Pittsburgh in 1965. The organization was an offshoot of the Frederic Ozanam Center, an African American community center sponsored by the Diocese of Pittsburgh and staffed by the Sisters of Charity until the 1970s. Sister Francis's orchestra performed with the likes of Maynard Ferguson, Harold Betters, and Count Basie in national venues such as Heinz Hall in Pittsburgh, Harlem's Apollo Theater, and Madison Square Garden. In addition, the Ozanam Strings produced two albums and toured in New Orleans and Canada. Many of the young musicians mentored by Sister Francis went on to become professional musicians in their adult life.

In July 1953, Sr. Marie Helene Mohr published her book *Saint Philomena, Powerful with God*. A newspaper article about the publication and Sr. Marie Helene's wish for a shrine to St. Philomena garnered numerous donations. Less than one year later, St. Philomena's Shrine, designed by Francis O'Connor Church, was dedicated on the highest knoll of the Seton Hill property. Hundreds of generous benefactors and businesses with a special devotion to St. Philomena supported the project. Unfortunately, the Vatican determined that St. Philomena was not a true saint, and her feast day was revoked in 1961. The shrine was closed that year.

Srs. Kathleen Delaney (left) and Regina Clare Breig (right) lead a candlelight processional to the Grotto of Lourdes at Seton Hill College as part of a women's retreat hosted by the sisters in the early 1960s. The sisters began conducting women's retreats in earnest during the 1940s. These retreats often encouraged young women to join the religious community or attend Seton Hill College. Additionally, these Seton Hill retreats allowed women to come closer to their own faith.

Mother Seton's spiritual descendants began convening in the 1940s to further Elizabeth Ann Seton's cause for canonization. By this time, independent communities in New York (1846); Cincinnati (1852); Halifax, Nova Scotia (1856); Convent Station, New Jersey (1859); and Greensburg (1870) had developed, in addition to the original community of Daughters of Charity in Emmitsburg, Maryland. Seen in this photograph are representatives from each of these Seton communities at the fourth conference of Mother Seton's Daughters in Mount St. Joseph, Ohio, in 1949. Mother Maria Benedict Monahan (second from left, seated) and Sr. Marie Agnes Reuber (second from left, standing) were the community representatives from Greensburg. The Sisters of Charity Federation, as it is now known, includes 13 religious congregations working collaboratively on behalf of the poor and marginalized around the world.

St. Vincent de Paul's special focus on the poor has continued through special ministries of the Sisters of Charity of Seton Hill during the past 150 years. Here, Sr. Carol Dougherty is supervising work at the food bank at St. Peter's Church in the South Side of Pittsburgh in the early 1990s.

Sr. Rosalie O'Hara was a pioneer in educational broadcasting. Sister Rosalie served as the director of the Quigley School of Communication Arts in Pittsburgh, coordinator of the Federation of Catholic High Schools, and chairwoman of Educational Television for the Catholic Schools of Pittsburgh. She wrote *Television Primer for Teachers* and produced a television series called *Alice in Poetryland* and a documentary, *The Life of Mother Seton*, for WQED in 1960. Here, Ed Sullivan presents Sister Rosalie with the Gold Bell Award from the Catholic Broadcasters Association for the documentary. She was also a charter member of the American Film Institute and the National Association of College Teachers in Film and Television. Sister Rosalie even traveled to Hollywood to study filmmaking at ABC TV Studios.

Pastoral ministry has been an important element of the Sisters of Charity ministries. Throughout the United States, the sisters have served as the face of local parishes. Sr. Leona Dolle (left) conducted home visits for Our Lady of Perpetual Help parish in Scottsdale, Arizona. Here, she visits Margaret and Arthur Heinson, who are in their 90s, to check on their well-being and give Communion.

The need for a large orphanage and maternity hospital in the city of Pittsburgh waned in the 1960s. In 1974, Phillip Murray Memorial, the former Roselia Foundling Hospital, became home to St. Joseph House of Hospitality, a facility for homeless men founded by the Catholic Radical Alliance in 1937 and continued by the St. Vincent De Paul Society. Here, Srs. Elizabeth Ann Stock (seated) and Marie Teresa Rishel are playing shuffle board with one of St. Joseph's residents in 1982.

During the Indo-China refugee crisis of 1975, the Sisters of Charity sponsored the family of Hoang Tan Ho (Joseph), a member of the South Vietnamese military who was evacuated out of Vietnam by the United States after the Fall of Saigon. The nine-member family had been settled at the refugee camp in Indiantown Gap, Pennsylvania. The children were enrolled in local schools, and the adults pursued educational and work opportunities. Sr. Sara Louise Reilly, pictured with Joseph and his wife, Mary, was the liaison for the sponsorship, and she kept in contact with the family through the years.

Ray O'Neil, Sister Elizabeth Ann Stock, Sister Marie Teresa Rishel, playing shuffle board, St. Joseph House of Hospitality, summer 1982

In 1975, Sr. Gemma del Duca (left) moved to Israel to work at Tel Gamaliel, a community for Jewish-Catholic dialogue. On a return visit to Greensburg in 1987, Sister Gemma approached Seton Hill College president Joanne Boyle with the idea to establish the National Catholic Center for Holocaust Education. With her cofounder, Sr. Mary Noel Kernan (right), Sister Gemma dedicated her life to encouraging Jewish-Catholic discourse and teaching the history of the Holocaust on an international scale. For her work, Sister Gemma has received the Elizabeth Seton Medal, the Elie Weisel Holocaust Remembrance Medal, the New Life Award, the Spirit of Anne Frank Award, and the Excellence in the Field of Holocaust Education Award given by Yad Vashem's International School for Holocaust Studies. She was the first non-Jew and non-Israeli to receive the Yad Vashem Award.

Creativity blossomed in the community of the Sisters of Charity. Many of the sisters became artists, designers, and published poets and authors. Sr. Mary Xavier Farrell was among the first young women to enter the community in Altoona in 1872. She published *Happy Memories of a Sister of Charity* in 1941. Sr. Fides Glass, a prolific painter and artist, illustrated the book that characterizes the founder, Mother Aloysia Lowe, and early community life.

On the very top of the hill was a level space.

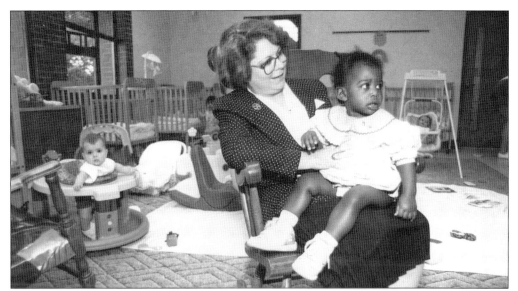

Elizabeth Seton Center, established in 1985 and adapted from the old Elizabeth Seton High School building, served first as a programming center for senior citizens in Allegheny County. Adult day-care programs became a focus of the center. Sr. Francis Assisi Gorham hosted the Seton Suzuki School of Music at the center. The facility became intergenerational when Sr. Mary Lucilla Wertz opened the children's day care. Sr. Barbara Ann Boss (pictured) became director of the children's program in 1988 and now serves as chief executive officer of the entire organization, which also provides after-school care and satellite programs in Westmoreland County.

Sr. Regina Marie Boslet served as the executive director of Campa Malta Center in Phoenix, Arizona, in the early 1990s. Founded in 1988, the Malta Center provided spiritual services, emotional support, physical services, social service programs, and educational opportunities to individuals infected and affected by HIV/AIDS. The organization was funded by the Order of Malta, an international organization of the Catholic Church, in addition to local Arizona charities.

The work of the Sisters of Charity of Seton Hill in prison ministry began in earnest in the 1970s. Sr. Mary Agnes Schildkamp taught general equivalency diploma (GED) courses and supported Operation Outward Reach, a work release and skill-development program, for inmates at State Correctional Institute (SCI), Greensburg. The 1980s saw Sr. Edith Strong conducting GED courses and helping with the Sunday liturgy, in addition to providing spiritual and emotional support to inmates and their families. In the 1990s, Sr. Eleanor Dillon (pictured) began Prison Network for female inmates. She served as a liaison between inmates and family, friends, and members of the criminal justice system, rehabilitation facilities, and other agencies.

Six

A LIFE OF HUMILITY, SIMPLICITY, AND CHARITY

The call to religious life comes in many different forms. In addition, the customs, definition of community, and daily ritual of each religious community varies. For the Sisters of Charity of Seton Hill, community has always been an essential component of daily life and contributes to the overall well-being of the individual sister and to the lifeblood of the congregation as a whole.

Orientation to the life of a sister begins with the novitiate, which is a formal period of training where the individual becomes accustomed to the demands of prayer, community, and service. Each sister plays a role in the running of the convent. The individual learns to share life in common with her sisters. Respecting and honoring individual differences, each sister moderates her own desires and wishes in the consideration of others. Professed sisters, those who have taken the vows of poverty, celibacy, and obedience, begin work in active ministry while upholding the lessons and routines from the novitiate.

Orientation into religious life and the discernment process have changed since Vatican II, but the essence remains the same.

For much of the history of the Sisters of Charity of Seton Hill, the congregation was governed solely by the mother superior while her councilors served as advisors. Within convents outside of the motherhouse, an individual sister was designated the "sister servant," which essentially meant that she managed the convent and served as the contact between the mother and the mission. Although the roles now function similarly, a more democratic system of living was encouraged after Vatican II.

Prayer, both private and communal, represents the soul of the congregation and allows the individual sister to connect with God.

Community life is a celebration of life. It includes the everyday effort to support and grow in love and appreciation for each other. The sisters enjoy the merriment of birthdays, anniversaries, special community days, honors, and graduations. Sisters share each other's difficulties and sorrows. They accompany one another at times of illness and deaths of family members and friends.

As the life of the sister closes, the community gathers in celebration of her life with prayer and music to accompany her on her final journey home.

In August 1932, the Sisters of Charity of Seton Hill celebrated 50 years since Mother Aloysia Lowe brought the community to Greensburg, Pennsylvania. In that 50 years, the community grew from 85 sisters to over 500. The Sisters of Charity posed in front of St. Mary's, the first motherhouse in Greensburg, formerly known as the Stokes mansion.

Education has always played an important role in the lives of the Sisters of Charity. The administration encouraged the sisters to pursue educational opportunities to further work in the missions and to enrich their lives. This group of novices from 1937–1938 and professed sisters poses at the entrance of Sullivan Hall for a class in Gregorian chant taught by Clifford A. Bennett in the summer of 1938.

In the summer of 1942, Srs. Mary Peter Murphy, M. Robert McManama, Marie George Abbott, M. Virginia Herald, M. Dorcas Smith, and Marie Gertrude McNeil studied aeronautics at St. Vincent College. These sisters received training to help with the war efforts.

Three sisters in the formation program for the Sisters of Charity, from left to right, Postulant Regina Ann (Mary Ralph) McKenzie; Sr. Mary Carl (Carla) Radermacher, novice; and Francis Xavier (Frances) Holland, young professed, stroll outside the motherhouse. Regina will spend six months as a postulant adjusting to the life, Sister Carla will have two novitiate years learning the rules and prayer life, and Sister Frances was just beginning a life in active ministry as a newly professed sister.

Six postulants stand in the novitiate sewing room as a senior novice, Sister Mary Carl, teaches them the fine points of sewing. All will begin to assemble the pieces for the habits they receive at reception to community. From left to right are Srs. Marie Bernard (Bernadine) Lauer, Aloysia O'Keefe, Mary Carl Radermacher, unidentified, Catherine Ann Zentner, Camillus Erb, and Mary Ralph McKenzie.

When the Sisters of Charity of Seton Hill become professed sisters, they must commit to first vows of poverty, obedience, chastity, and charity and sign a card indicating their commitment to these vows. This photograph from August 1964 shows a group of newly professed sisters signing their vow card alongside the then-current mother superior, Mother M. Victoria Brown (seated center), and Sr. Theodosia Murtha (seated right). Also shown are Srs. Marian Seton McCauley, Mary Jo Mutschler, Judith Marie McKenna, Patricia Laffey, Louise de Paul Burke, Deborah Anne Moore, and Jeannine Connelly.

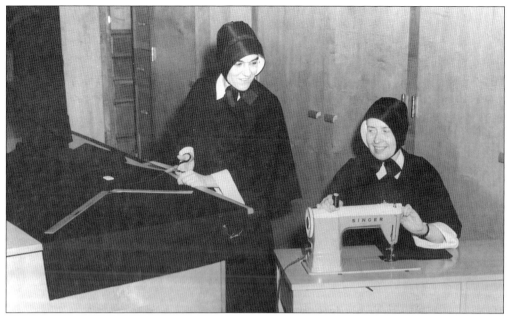

Srs. Mary Carl (Carla) Radermacher (left) and Placide (Marjorie) Flanagan (right) prepare habits in the Clothes Room in Assumption Hall. The Clothes Room was the department store for clothes for the sisters. Twice a year, each sister ordered the items needed. Orders for everything from a new habit to a white cotton nightgown were available. The day the packages arrived on each mission was somewhat like Christmas.

In this undated photograph, several sisters pray before the exposition of the Blessed Sacrament in the chapel at Assumption Hall. The chapel was the design of Sr. Mary Francis Irvin. Sister designed the monstrance pictured below the crucifix. The Sisters of Charity often hold exposition of the Blessed Sacrament on the first Friday of every month.

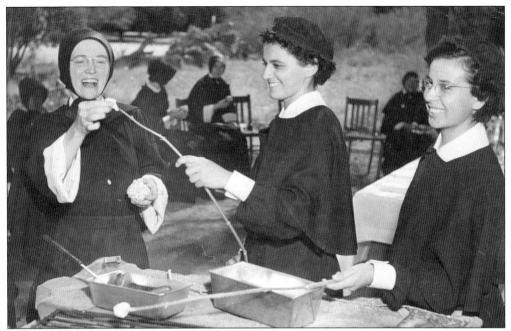

During the early 1950s, Sr. Jean Agnes (Irene) Fallon takes a marshmallow from a stick held by Ramona Felix (Sr. Mary Ramon) as Consuelo Pacheco (Sr. Maria Consuelo) toasts another marshmallow in Tucson, Arizona. Ramona and Consuelo became postulants at Casa Elizabeth Seton in Tucson on September 8, 1953. They received the habit in Greensburg in 1954.

Music plays an important role in the lives of the sisters, not only enhancing prayer but also for recreation. Sisters assigned to Immaculate Conception Convent in Irwin in 1950 gather around Sr. Evangeline O'Donnell at the piano for a sing-a-long. From left to right are Srs. Mary Aiden Geary, Mary Jean Dolan, Rose Agnes McGowan, Alice Louise (Mildred) Corvi, Mary Jude McColligan, Mary Paul Coleman, and Francis de Sales Joyce.

In gingham aprons, the sisters in Cathedral Convent prepare the Silver Jubilee dinner for Srs. Miriam Ruth Clark and Richard Ann Watson on September 29, 1959. Sr. LaSalette Hayes holds the first plate as Sr. Felicita Diggin serves. From left to right, Srs. Anicita Gibson, Paul Marie (Marie Teresa) Rishel, and Sebastian Jellison wait their turn. Sr. Zachary Endress stirs the pot. Partially hidden in the picture is Patty Lynam, daughter of Tom Lynam, photographer for the occasion.

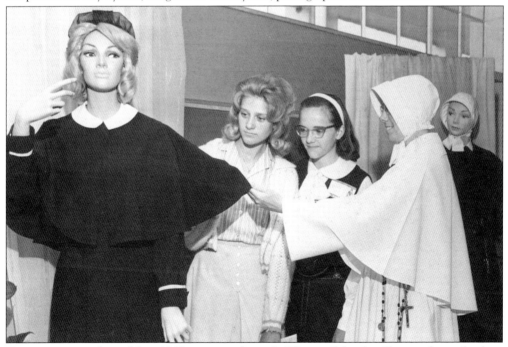

Two mannequins dressed for a 1960s vocation day at St. Theresa School in Phoenix depict the dress worn during the first stages of formation. Sr. Mary Philip Aaron describes the postulant dress to two interested students. The white-cap novice habit is on the far right. The mannequins appear a bit too modern for the postulants and novices of the day, but the clothing is authentic.

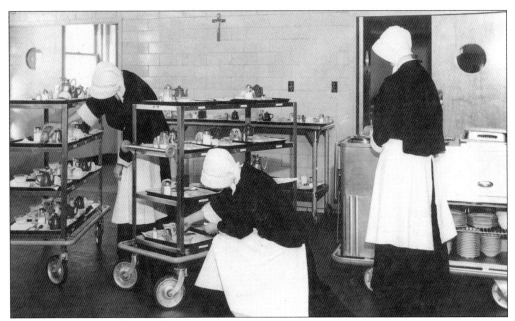

The novices who resided in the Ennis Hall Novitiate adjacent to Assumption Hall prepare the trays for infirm sisters in the kitchen during the spring of 1955. Novices assisted in the kitchen, dining room, laundry, and housekeeping. The day of a novice included early rising, morning and evening prayer, meditation, a time of adoration before the Blessed Sacrament, Mass, and prayers throughout the day, along with everyday chores and some recreation.

During the summer of 1972, several buses and cars drove up the mountain on Route 40 to carry many members of the Sisters of Charity to a summer community day at Marymount in the Laurel Mountains of Pennsylvania. Marymount, a gift of Fr. Owen J. Kirby, was a beautiful, isolated property with a stone house, pool, and a chapel designed by architect Carlton Strong. Mother Richard Ann Watson (smiling at the camera) joins in the fun as Sr. Judith Marie McKenna (left) and several others share in the camaraderie and good spirits.

Originally named the Novitiate Building, Doran Hall was built in 1963 as a house of formation for the Sisters of Charity. It was renamed in 1970 after Mother Josephine Doran, the third mother superior of the community. Queen of Peace Chapel (pictured) was designed by Celli-Flynn Brennan Architects & Planners in Pittsburgh as the center of prayer in the new novitiate. The interior appointments were created by George Nakashima, a world-renowned Japanese American craftsman. In 2012, Queen of Peace Chapel received the American Institute of Architects Timeless Award.

The Sisters of Charity of Seton Hill held a large festival on the grounds every summer from 1954 until it discontinued after the 1984 event. Sr. Brigid Marie Grandey looks happy as she prepares the sweets for the popular candy booth for the summer festival of 1961. The booth, featuring homemade fudge, caramels, and bonbons made by volunteer sisters under the tutelage of Sr. Rose Angela Cunningham, was the most popular on the campus. At the end of the festival, the shelves were bare.

During the 1960s, Mother Victoria Brown took great pride in the summer festival booth she sponsored called Wall Street. Margaret Garrity, a Seton Hill alumna and faculty member and volunteer, stands beside Mother Victoria. Sr. Mary Eustace Mullen surveys the options and awaits service. This booth contained the most valuable prizes available during the festival. At the end of the last evening, Bernard Scherer, a faculty member, was auctioneer for a fun auction on the lawn.

Following the changes in habit after Vatican II, the Sisters of Charity of Seton Hill gathered in St. Joseph Chapel on June 19, 1977, to receive the symbol and ring worn by all community members. Sr. Sara Louise Reilly (left), assisted by Sr. Mary Francis Irvin who designed the symbol, hands Sr. Ann Louise Sacco her treasure. Srs. Mary Janet Ryan (second from right) and Isabelle Jorden (right) wait in line.

Mother Richard Ann Watson witnesses Sr. Baptista Madden's acceptance as leader of the Sisters of Charity of Seton Hill at the Mass of Installation in June 1977. Sr. Baptista Madden was the first elected superior to continue to use the title sister rather than the designation Mother. Sisters elect new leadership teams every five years during the congregation's general chapter meeting.

The cemetery at Seton Hill holds significance to the Sisters of Charity who gather for private visits, prayer services, and burials for the sisters who have completed their earthly journey. All of the sisters in the US province are buried in the cemetery planned by Mother Aloysia Lowe, who was the second sister buried there. All of the Seton Hill University presidents, some former employees, and other significant persons have places in this "holy ground." (Courtesy of Sr. Hyun-me Kim.)

About the Sisters of Charity of Seton Hill

The Sisters of Charity of Seton Hill is an international, apostolic community of women religious, baptized in Christ and vowed to continue the mission of His Church. In the spirit of St. Vincent de Paul and St. Elizabeth Seton, the congregation conceives its purpose to be an active ministry on behalf of His Kingdom. This service is informed by Gospel values, responsive to the needs of a changing world, guided by the prudent use of available resources, respectful of human dignity, protective of human rights, devoted especially to the poor and oppressed, rooted in faith, animated by prayer, supported by the common life, and performed in humility, simplicity, and charity.

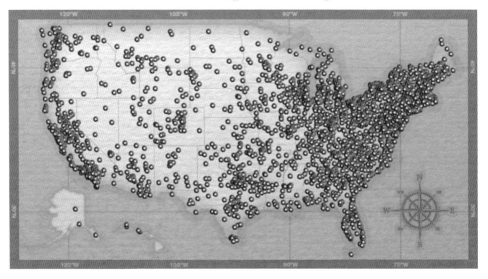